# DON'T STARTUP

## WHAT NO ONE TELLS YOU ABOUT STARTING YOUR OWN BUSINESS

# KARTHIK KUMAR

*To MAHA.*

*DREAM.*
*FLY.*

*2019.*

**notion**press
.com

INDIA · SINGAPORE · MALAYSIA

# Notion Press

Old No. 38, New No. 6
McNichols Road, Chetpet
Chennai - 600 031

First Published by Notion Press 2018
Copyright © Karthik Kumar 2018
All Rights Reserved.

ISBN 978-1-64429-186-3

*This book is* dedicated to *01CM01.*


*Thank you for letting me know something that only my silent soul could have known – that there were books inside me. This is the first one. I may have written it, but you planted the seed and have coaxed its harvest. I owe you plenty.*

# Contents

# Act II

# Act III

# Acknowledgements

Thank you for being the family to Evam- Mom, Dad, Sunil, Sunil's Mom and Dad, Preethi, Pavithra and Suchi.

Thank you, Ramkumar, for teaching us about flight.

Thank you to all the entrepreneurs who we met on the way and wished we could meet on the way. All of you inspired us.

Thanks to those who stood by Evam through everything- Kaushik Palicha, Divyesh Palicha, TR Santhanakrishnan, Kiran Reddy, Hanif Sattar, Suhail Sattar, Mukund Padmanabhan, Nina Reddy, Alexander Zach, Sunil Handa, RU Srinivas, Opn, Red Letter and all our employees.

# Introduction

May our story unfold in three Acts, like all great drama.

In Act I, I will tell you about all the challenges and dilemmas of a startup in its 'infant' startup phase – the years of learning to stand on one's own feet while getting ready to face the world. Evam stayed in this phase longer than most startups – owing to the inexperience of the founders and also the non-existence of a ready ecosystem in India for the nature of our business.

I wish someone had guided us during this period. But we did receive some guidance from many well-meaning seniors in our world, and also like *Eklavya*, we learnt from many gurus from a distance. The spirit of *Don't Startup* is to share this wisdom with you, because the wisdom is best valued when it is passed on and shared further.

In Act II, I will get into the 'adolescent' phase of a startup – the awkward years of getting to know yourself and putting yourself out there, and being unsure, while trying to seem confident and unfazed.

This was also a longer period for Evam compared to other startups because of the lack of any direct competitors who could help us build a market. Lots of people said we did not have any competition and called it our 'blue ocean strategy.' I often lamented that maybe no one else saw the opportunity we did and in that doubt-ridden period this seemed to make us seem too hopeful and maybe even deluded.

We failed the most in this period. Hence I talk of the various difficulties we faced because of our failures, and worse, our successes!

In Act III, I will reflect on the coming-of-age years – when we could no longer call ourselves a startup, but we were still handling image and operational issues that emanated from our long startup phase.

In this section, I will handle the 'bigger picture' issue, the vision and how to set your sights on the future.

I will periodically reflect on *qualities* of an entrepreneur. Qualities that one needs to have or hone and EQ challenges that one should always be aware of in the journey.

In the course of this book, you will get to hear the story of my startup journey with Evam. Read it like a fable, for that is what it is, to you – it's only a reality for me. But I have used that fable to talk about what it means to *you* and your startup because tomorrow is yours, and your startup will be your responsibility.

You are your dream, and this book is more about your dream than my reality – more about your future, than my past.

Karthik Kumar,

**Entrepreneur**

# Act I

Chapter 1

# The Why

"Why does Bruce Wayne bother being Batman?"

It was 2001. I was 23, with a degree in engineering, which ensured social validity, and a degree in Brand Management and Marketing Communications that gave me employability. I was one month away from graduating and 12 hours away from submitting my combined thesis on the 'Viability of a Theatre/Drama based entertainment entrepreneurship.'

Combined theses were rare. Two students are allowed to work collaboratively on one thesis. It was my classmate, Sunil Vishnu and me – credited to be the founders of the Theatre and Amateur Drama movement 'Sankalp' at MICA, the marketing school we went to. Our director allowed us this privilege after an impassioned plea, PowerPoint slides, micro notes et al., made by the two of us for the board of directors of the school.

The results were being typed out as our thesis – the dot matrix printer chugged, which I was convinced, was going to delay our graduation by a further month.

The results weren't good.

We had traveled across cities in India and spoken to theatre practitioners, filmmakers, ad film production houses, drama repertories, performing arts venue heads, and even to venture capitalists and investors. They were all curious, concerned and mildly discouraging, without meaning to be.

'It has never been done,' they said and it surely hadn't been done without a benevolent arts funding. It wasn't sustainable. The world was moving away, even then, from watching live performing arts and drama to more electronic (not yet digital) solutions. It could be glorious but only as a hobby.

We didn't have entrepreneurship in our blood neither did we have the arts. Our parents belonged to the working middle class and they had given us meaningful educational degrees as inheritances, and a bunch of value systems that would ensure a respectable future.

Daring to take a chance and learning new skills were luxuries and not those we could ever afford easily. Our exposure to arts was limited to painting and drawing classes at school, and the occasional school drama directed by the English teacher. Arts as a means of living was meant for the children of artists – be it the traditional arts or even the more commercial ones like cinema. Most businesses in India are family businesses.

Business acumen, artistic pedigree and entitlement to follow these streams are passed down through genes, according to the Indian mindset.

I held the printouts of the thesis in my hand – hot ink drying on silken A4 sheets. It read, in Ariel font and in Bold, 'A theatre/drama based entertainment entrepreneurship will not be viable.' It will never be a sustainable business and even finding this out would require deep pockets and generous benevolent funding, just to see it through a few generations.

Campus placements were round the corner, and honestly, we had some sweet jobs lined up for ourselves that would give us respectable lives...

The results were clear – Don't Startup!

## Bruce Wayne and Batman

Why does Bruce Wayne bother being Batman?

The need to be Batman says a lot about why Bruce Wayne does what he does. The backstory of his parents being killed, which results in a lifetime of avenging their death, is nothing but character building. But the serious commitment to convert a fleeting encounter with bats into a Batsuit, Batmobile, Batcave and an entire underground Bat enterprise that seeks to save an entire city is almost emotionally cathartic or unstable – depending on which side of marveling him you are.

The Batsuit is exciting. The Batmobile turns heads. The Bat weapons are cool. The Bat-signal is a shiny signal of validation! Bruce Wayne is fine by himself – but Batman is what the movies are made of.

Replace the Batsuit with your own chosen battle outfit or the need to conform or not conform and the Bat-signal with a cool designation, company logo and a visiting card. Add a desk, a workspace and an entire enterprise that functions at your calling to the mix and create your batcave. Hire as many Alfreds as you will. And you can become the Dark Knight!

Today, entrepreneurship is seen as a great way to feel invincible while you're still mortal. We feel like a vigilante trying to set right what we see as a problem in the world/market/society and we go about it with a sense of enterprise and we certainly don't want to remain anonymous doing it. We want to leave our footprint. We want the Bat-signal, the Gotham tribute – we want the platitudes and the validation that goes with the drama of journeying it alone.

We live in a world where people like Steve Jobs are celebrated every day and the anonymous corporate and its invisible worker-ant are ignored – sometimes even ridiculed. But the sexiness and the promise of social validation is a trap. Ask yourself this, what is it about this entrepreneur avatar that excites you? Is it the Batsuit and the perks or is it the invisible thousands of hours of work, labour and uncertainty that lie ahead.

Does this seem exciting to you in absolute terms or only relatively, when you compare it to a corporate job where you'll be taking instructions, as opposed to giving instructions in an entrepreneurial 'boss' role? The journey is like any other and maybe more difficult – filled with great uncertainty all the time with a requirement of 100% of your effort at every point. Money, knowledge, fame are all hard to come by in a measure that you will consider enough, or at least sustainable. And no one will love your Batsuit as much you do, and the fact that it fits perfectly will remain a feeling that you will be unable to fully share with any other.

So, how much of your need to be an entrepreneur is actually only a need to feel important? We submitted the thesis. The thesis successfully made it clear that we should not delve into this venture, even in theory. But we didn't accept the results.

We vowed to startup after two years because we needed seed capital. Our jobs and salaries would pay back our educational loans, and help us get the seed capital ourselves. We sat for placements. We got good respectable jobs that paid us well. Our 2-year countdown had begun.

2 years of waking up in dingy bachelor pads in congested cities. Doing sales, but calling it marketing, because it sounded more strategic. Every day was a blur of logistics. The life of a sales exec is similar to the life of a foot soldier in the army – you will be sent first, everywhere and sent all the time. Ensuring one's daily livelihood stayed under the budget of the 'per diem' was the only tactical win every day. And whenever I felt like giving up, I reminded myself of the two-year countdown.

Cut to 2003. I was 25, and Evam was born. So why did we start up? Why did we 'Evam?' Evam was born out of the need to be significant.

Even the name 'Evam' came from this need. 'Evam,' the name came from the play 'Evam Indrajit' ('And Indrajit'). The play was set in newly-independent India, when the initial promise of freedom had lost its shine, and the entire system had become a mere Indian version of the British machinery of *babu-dom* and bureaucracy. India's youth had earned freedom without knowing the consequences of freedom. We were like an unchained circus elephant that chose to remain in the circus, because it didn't know any other way.

Indrajit was that bolt out of the blue, that spark amidst dull skies, the unique rat that was running into the sinking ship, sensing 'opportunity.' In that quest for significance, 'Evam' was born.

We wanted to give ourselves a chance. We wanted to make the journey memorable for ourselves. We didn't want any regrets. We wanted to make all of it count.

The fact that Evam set out to be an entrepreneurship in the management of the live performing arts was also unique, because there was no such thing in India, and the closest known cousins to the species were 'Event Management' or 'Theatre as a Hobby.'

There is an innate need in an entrepreneur to stop the traffic and get noticed. There is a need in an entrepreneur to say no to existing processes and forcibly offer a different way.

# Takeouts

- Today, even if you're not an entrepreneur, when startups are the norm, the need for significance will still exist in the DNA of a potential entrepreneur, but it will manifest itself in many ways in operations, branding and solution-ing or even in creating organizational culture.

- Every entrepreneur will seek to make his own Batcave. But before that you should stop and ask yourself, why be Batman at all? Why not just remain Bruce Wayne? Why entrepreneurship? Why not intra-preneurship within a steady job? Maybe you'll better off if you don't startup?

- Anyway, your need to be significant may be only the initial fuel to power the decision to get started into entrepreneurship, but you need to understand that it takes much more than that to keep the flame alive. It helps to learn early on that what is in front of you is many hours, and even years, of invisible labour and toil, and struggles, which no one will ever get to know of, or bother to write platitudes about.

- Even this book is being written by me about my own journey! One could say I have *entre-pruned* this book as well.

## Why do *you* want to startup?

Write down your answer on a blank page. You will need to hear yourself answer this one.

And I assure you these will be the most difficult words you will ever write if they have to convince you and the world around you. This is your mission statement. The WHY of starting up!

And if you feel like you dropped a nugget of truth on that empty page and feel like sharing it with someone who would understand, write me an email with your mission statement to kk@evam.in. I'll be happy to hear from you. But don't start up without doing this!

Chapter 2

# The What

"Entrepreneurship is not just short term advantage, it is long term resilience."

But what should my startup be about? What should I be an entrepreneur in? You could be struggling with this...

The Evam answer to 'what should we do' was too simple.

Evam's 'reason to be' was a spirit, a quest for significance, as well as a need to convert 'what we loved doing' into a product offering and make a living for ourselves. That's why, I often think, we are equal parts the spirit, and the product. Because the big questions were, 'Would we have joined an organization then, in a job that would have given us a ready platform and the monetary appreciation for our talents?' I don't think so. 'Would we have started up just about anything then, if we had had ready access to funds and resources?' Surely not.

We were what most entrepreneurs tend to be – single-minded and obstinate. We wanted to do what we wanted to do, and we wanted to do it our way. We knew we wanted to make a living doing what we loved doing so we were willing to do whatever it took to realize that. And at the same time we wanted to go on own our journey – we were willing to listen, but we wanted the responsibility of our reactions. But what should your startup idea be? That could be a challenging dilemma...

Let us explore the various kinds of startups.

## The various kinds of startups

### Simplest is the product/solution idea – the Invention Startup

Someone comes up with a solution to a problem in the world out there, and is willing to spend hours solving the problem. How quickly this solution can reach the market defines the success of this kind of venture. This entrepreneur will need full support during incubation and meanwhile systems have to be geared up for delivering to the market. Timing is of essence, because there is very little of it.

In this kind of startup, the entrepreneur may see themselves as an inventor first and a business person after.

The question these entrepreneurs have to ask themselves in this case is will they have any entrepreneurship left in them in case their invention fails?

## The next one is the Entrepreneur's Entrepreneur

Someone who clearly says that they don't want to work for anyone else and want to be the master of their own destiny so they're willing to commit to the journey. They will be on the lookout for the next ship to sail. They will be attracted to ideas and see which one they can latch themselves on to.

In this case the idea becomes critical, since latching on was already a foregone conclusion. Find an idea that you can genuinely contribute to, not just in terms of funding, but also to the development of. Otherwise you may just become a CEO of the enterprise where you make all venture decisions but have no control over the product development ones. This could inhibit your need to be master of your destiny.

In the classic Apple example, Woz was the inventor startup, and Jobs was the entrepreneur's entrepreneur. I call them by their second names because I'm pretentious like that. Woz had little interest in the entrepreneurial part of the journey, and Jobs had lesser interest in product development. Jobs learnt the skill he lacked and Woz didn't! Jobs stayed the course.

**Next is the 'Get Rich Quick' Startup Entrepreneur**

They will monitor trends and quickly put together a vehicle that can run the race, stay ahead of the curve, just enough to get attention, and then get bought out. This book has little wisdom for this kind of entrepreneur. *Don't Startup* sees entrepreneurship as a lifelong committed journey, and not as a speed dating program. Although that is also a valid identity – being a Serial Entrepreneur.

A serial entrepreneur's need to startup is compulsive. They will quickly put something together and start it and they will be onto their next venture, whether they are settled in or not.

**Then there is the Curious Entrepreneur**

They have equal curiosity for entrepreneurship and ideas. Whatever they are active consumers of, will interest them, and they will try and see how they could venture into something that they would be an active consumer of. You will find foodies becoming restaurateurs, gamers becoming game developers and movie directors becoming production house owners. This journey is one of constant learning - both on the product and on the entrepreneurship front.

So then the question remains – what kind of startup should yours be? Here is an approach...

## Organic Curiosity

Considering that being an entrepreneur takes a significant measure of your energy in your life, it becomes important to decide what it is that you are going to be a startup in.

It can be confusing if you are interested in many things and have many startup ideas. Having many startup ideas is like having no singular gripping startup idea.

And next, is there an idea at all, and if so what is it? Or is it just a product/service that already exists and you also want to be a part of that space. For instance, opening yet another fast food joint in your area! It may not be the first fast food joint, but it's certainly 'your' first fast food joint.

These are questions that can paralyze you into inaction and inertia. And not asking this question could mean you start up with something quickly and also lose interest in it just as quickly. Let me clarify this decision-making process for you.

What do you spend hours and hours doing without caring about how much time you're spending on it? What is that topic or subject that makes you jump into a conversation each time it is being discussed, and has you chatting on and on about it until someone requests you to shut up? What is that subject that you lose yourself in, googling it until your laptop runs out of charge and you find that need to plug it in again? What do you have the most opinions about? And the most evolved opinions about? For some of my classmates and peers this was cricket or even gaming, and believe me some of them have found a calling in those fields. They have become opinion leaders, consultants and even entrepreneurs.

You are actually unique – be it your DNA, your physical appearance, your mental makeup and personality. The leaves of a tree may appear alike, until you realize that each one is distinctly different from the other. In fact, no two leaves of a tree are alike! You may be forced to run the same race as others, but there is a chance that you will run it your way, have a different plan and run, do your own post run analysis and celebrate your victory differently. It becomes your responsibility to find that thing you are most interested in and organically curious about. This will lead to greater self-knowledge and awareness and that will lead to greater fulfillment and joy.

And if you find your startup in this space, closest to your *Organic Curiosity*, then I can assure you a life of great joy. Like those hours that raced past you while you were in the pursuit of your passion, so will the years in your life – they will be filled with purpose, and involvement and will surely be worth remembering, for yourself.

Will it make money? Will it be successful? Is it the best idea? All this will depend on how good a leader and captain you turn out to be. Leadership is a skill that you will have to get better at, until you can hire someone better than you.

But you will be the best person to realize this idea, because of your natural involvement and passion in the space. Whatever you are most curious and excited about, you will also learn more about. You will always have enough knowledge because your curiosity will drive you to learn more. Even if you are the fourth fast food joint in your own area, you may be the most serious and committed and passionate brand, and will certainly outlive the others due to your love for the product/service.

Imagine building a castle, a fortress and an entire kingdom around something that you yourself quickly lose interest in? Instead, find something you love doing and even a hut around it will feel like a castle.

Follow your Organic Curiosity. Let your startup reflect who you are. Evam was a curiosity entrepreneurship. We were driven into a field we were organically curious about and also in a way (entrepreneurially) that we were curious about it. We knew neither theatre/drama nor entrepreneurship.

It was through the Evam journey that we learnt leadership and even honed our entire work-related skill of theatre and drama. We neither learnt the skill nor entrepreneurship, formally. We only had the eagerness to know more, and the naïveté to make mistakes and not feel at fault.

What Evam does: We believe in the spirit of endeavour, in keeping that spirit alive and alight. We believe life is too short to be spent doing things that you don't love doing, or believe in. We believe you deserve to love your labour, and should labour to love what you do. We believe in entrepreneurship. We believe in the value of the moment and that the moments that lie ahead need to be filled with valuable experiences. That value must be created. We believe in making it memorable, for you and for ourselves. We believe in the performing arts. We are 'Evam.'

Nine out of ten startups fail. What made us succeed? Assuming that success means staying on course, not folding up, staying in pursuit with hope and energy – while depending only on ourselves.

We enjoyed the learning process. We enjoyed succeeding. We didn't fear failure as much as we respected it. And mostly we defined success to be this – staying in pursuit to making a living from doing what we enjoy doing, and doing what it takes in order to be able to live respectfully on our own terms. So were we successful? Yes, according to how we defined it for ourselves. Still are. Do we now know entrepreneurship and are we the best at our skill of product? No.

# Takeouts

- Reflect on what kind of startup you are – the invention startup, entrepreneur's entrepreneur, get rich startup, serial entrepreneur, curious entrepreneur and get the appropriate help required. Different startups require different partners.

- It is okay to not know the subject or the very nature of entrepreneurship, but it's important that you remain passionately interested in the subject, and in learning how to be a better entrepreneur. This journey is one of constant learning – both on the product front and on the entrepreneurship front.

- *Entrepreneurship is not just short-term advantage, it is long-term resilience.*

- Find your organic curiosity.

## Here is a simple exercise.

This may require you to look back at your life in retrospect and find out what those few subjects are that has always kept you interested passionately. Talk to your close friends, your parents, and even favorite teachers, about the things that you have been consistently interested in and what they noticed about you when you were doing those things. This reflection will help you understand not only the 'what' but also 'how' passionate you have been about it, and why that subject has interested you.

*Follow your Organic Curiosity. Let your startup reflect who you are.*

Chapter 3

# Time

"A lot of starting up is waiting - waiting uncertainly, waiting endlessly and waiting without knowing what it is that you are actually waiting for."

The phase 1 of Evam's journey was much like Bruce's journey as Batman. Overnight, our lives were filled with a sense of purpose. And the feeling of filling one's day with activities that were oriented to realizing our own vision and whims was almost self-actualizing.

Between 2003–05 every single activity, from replacing the light bulb to moving the bed to make into a workspace, to getting our own visiting cards designed, was one more step towards changing the world, our world. The press found new, multiple excuses to write about us. People read what the press wrote about, took them seriously and then took us seriously. It felt good to be taken seriously.

Simple questions became paramount – what do we wear for a meeting that says something about ourselves, what do we leave behind, what's the nature of our conversation, how do we communicate and make an impression. If we were to name ourselves, what would we call ourselves and who would we be?

Our logo design and its place on our card were challenges that took us long hours and typesets and yes, we didn't have a designer for that first logo, nor the budget for one. People were watching our smallest steps and we felt important. This sense of validation was a trap, because everything new was shiny, had a scent to it and had our eagerness and anticipation written all over it. Beyond tearing open the gift wrapping, what remains of the gift, the week after Christmas?

We were to find out very soon that people were going to care lesser and lesser. The story was going to go around quickly enough and everybody had already heard it, and heard it enough! Customers move onto the next shiny thing, and you get to go along, or you get left behind, but either way you won't hear from them as much, in the form of eulogies or even loud criticism. It'll almost seem like they have stopped caring but that won't be entirely true. The need for validation will stop very soon, and the traffic will resume. But therein will lie the greatest nemesis an Entrepreneur will face for all time - Time!

## Time is (not) on your side...

Batman Begins was the first part of what would become a filmmaker's three-part masterpiece, the Dark Knight trilogy.

But I always had a problem with that movie. It didn't do anything for me when I watched it for the first time. I hardly saw Batman or the Batsuit. I was wondering what he was doing so far away from the action. There was no love interest or supervillains, and almost no plot either. It felt too long and all Batman was doing was starting up.

Most of entrepreneurship in the beginning, the startup phase, will be about negotiating time. The biggest enemy of the infant startup will be the hurry and the sense of urgency that has driven the founders into starting up. But nothing will get done as quickly as you would like it to, and worse, if it gets done quickly and urgently it won't be done so good. Everything will get far more delayed than you would be comfortable with. And that delay would have been okay and bearable if you were fully occupied – but that won't be the case. The delay would mean rediscovering your opposable thumbs and re-inventing the twiddle.

A lot of starting up is waiting – waiting uncertainly, waiting endlessly and waiting without knowing what it is that you are actually waiting for. Time won't be on your side because you will have lots of it. And the cruelest conundrum would be people assuming you are a lot busier than you actually will be. You won't be that busy. So you will feel compelled to create busy-ness.

Busy-ness is the compulsive need to appear like one is useful, being purposeful and always active. There is a sense of coolness associated with being busy, as if the agenda has already been laid out before you, and is only awaiting you. And all you do is walk in and get things done, one after the other, until they all get done. And then when it is all done, the next set of activities present themselves.

Busy-ness is an urban disease because a person who doesn't appear busy seems like a gigantic loser, especially if he doesn't have the swag of saintliness about him. Busy-ness is what will get your neighbour uncle to leave you alone. Otherwise he will feel like you have the time for the 'life lessons' that he would like to share with you whether he has your consent or not, he will assume you have the time!

2003 was our launch year – we kicked off operations in April, and we delivered our first project 6 months thereafter. 6 months isn't long now that we look back upon it. But we did not know or realize that the end of the 6th month would see us delivering our first project. So the time period was uncertain. Those 6 months seemed excruciatingly long since we were seeking funders for a big project (in the arts we used to call it sponsorship – something we realized was a toxic source of funding later on – which we shall discuss later!). So it was a question of chicken and egg and clearly whichever came first, our project was the one that came after both egg and chicken! In those 6 months I used to do accounts and I don't mean I used to account for expenses in order to maintain order.

I used to do accounts obsessively. That aspect of the business was not my strength so I used to overcompensate by doing it, redoing it, undoing everything and doing it all over again – generally overdoing it! Until I knew every last paisa was balanced and we knew where the money was going.

My middle-class mindset also told me that it was all going and going fast. And it was. The more I did accounts the more smaller problems seemed like bigger problems. Did doing accounts give us perspective? Yes, but only when it was done periodically! Not when it was done compulsively and obsessively. Did doing it this way contribute to busy-ness? Yes, certainly. Did it contribute to business? No!

The other thing we used to do was what I call meeting fatigue, where everyone gathered to discuss everything. It used to feel like we were all in sync because we all felt connected and somehow this seemed democratic and exciting. But what did it achieve? Beyond a sense of togetherness, pretty much nothing. For the sake of busy-ness a little enterprise was behaving like a large one, only because appearing busy was so important. Therefore we were mimicking larger organizations and their culture, without realizing that maybe that this wasn't serving ours any purpose.

I'm not saying don't do too many meetings, I'm saying we were tempted to discuss everything every time with everyone, because we had all the time and nothing much to do. This didn't help much when we got truly busy and teams felt paralyzed when they didn't have that much time anymore to discuss and meet because this had inadvertently become our culture.

# Takeouts

- Don't link busy-ness to your self-worth!

  You will wake up and fill the day's to-do list and if you don't you will feel like a loser and your mind will wander wistfully towards your peers who all appear to be doing so much and moving so fast. A day ahead of you with nothing much to do will seem like a nightmare.

  Be aware of this, being busy is not always good for business.

- Busy-ness has a very delicate relationship with business.

  There is an optimum level of busy-ness that is good for business – any lesser than that could be harmful and any more than that will certainly be harmful and unproductive.

  Only being busy doing the right things contributes to business.

- You will try and busy yourself more, be aware of that.

  I'll tell you that busy-ing yourself won't help much but you won't listen because the restlessness will eat into you. So go ahead and busy yourself, but not too much. Don't be so busy that when things start actually moving, you are too occupied to notice or react. If you have too much time, then get busy practicing or

# Takeouts

training, or even better, staying silent and staying stage-ready.

Or just take up a hobby or a sport that will help you socialize and network with your immediate world. All the people you play with and share interests with will become business contacts and aides, I assure you. Because the secret is this, people do business with people they like and are familiar with. To most people, YOU are the business. So go out there and spend time networking through a hobby/sport.

## Here is an exercise that will help.

Every business has many facets- finance, HR, accounts, marketing, selling, product, logistics etc. Pick the department you have least exposure to, or are least interested in. And with the time available, instead of artificially creating busy-ness, deep dive into learning this aspect that you are the weakest in. You may never become an expert at it, but I assure you that your knowledge of it will certainly become a strong point for you later. At least you will not fear what you don't know – the feeling of relative familiarity will prevent you from being inhibited about it. Use this time to learn that!

# Chapter 4

# Money

"Time is the only currency that you have."

How much money is enough money to startup? How much seed capital does one need?

This is a profound question that can stump any wannabe startup because there is no precise mathematical calculation for this. I have seen many young potential startups not startup, because they haven't gotten enough funding yet. And if you are a startup without ready funding from an entity, or have not come from big wealth, then I fully understand how it becomes critical to compute this sum of enough that will decide whether you are ready to startup or not. But enough is never enough!

- 'Enough' is a middle-class malady.

We believe we are experts at defining enough and living within our means. But the truth is that our definition of enough is expandable and it keeps changing with the times. What is enough for now will become different tomorrow and will only keep expanding, like the universe.

So if you decide a sum as 'enough' seed capital to startup, then if you let time go by, that sum will expand to occupy a bigger volume.

- This is not inflation, this is inertia.

  Your mind is creating an infinity loop to prevent you from doing the tough job of putting yourself out there and finding out the truth about your startup idea and effort.

- Money has more sentimental value to the middle-class mindset than any other.

  Upper-class people have to handle abundance and lower class people have to always be content without much. But middle-class people hold onto whatever they have as if it won't ever come back if it ever left them.

Evam was started with a seed capital of Rs. 1,00,000 and initially as a partnership firm. (later converted into a private limited). We had a reserve of around Rs 2,00,000 in our bank accounts – a line of credit from ourselves to

Evam, also known as savings. This was the outcome of 2 years of saving up from the salaries we were making from our campus placement jobs. We scrounged and lived like rats. We made tours and saved on the per diems. We ate cheaper than our HR-band allowed us and billed marginally higher than actuals and saved the difference. We didn't buy our first anything- bike, video game, TV, gifts for parents... nothing. Was this sum enough to start Evam?

## Show me the money...

How emotional should one get about money? What is its value? Money on its own has no value, until you have some use for it. Its value is linked to what it's being used for and therefore brings into focus what it is being used for.

The truth will be that one will never have 'enough' money in the startup phase and this will seem like a curse, and you will be tempted to look at other businesses, peers and marvel at how green the grass is on their manicured lawns. The truth is also that, in the startup phase, it's best not to have more than enough funds. Because when things are uncomfortable, money becomes a quick fix. Money can buy you solutions, the best people, systems and even customers. All this will be fine for initial bottom lines, but it will create a placebo, which when removed, will cause things to not work as well as before. Lack of money, on the other hand, will lead to sharper thinking – efficiency seeking, forging bonds with suppliers that will lead to more meaningful conversations than 'how much,' more work on shaping prototype without the option of creating a mould that will make more of the same.

They say that time is money and most often one would never understand what that means – if time was money why could we not encash it, especially in the startup phase of infinite time and very finite money! But the truth is time is the only currency that you have now. Therefore, you have to see how time can be made into money. Simple, by using the time!

Take longer to find the right partners, suppliers, talent. Spend more time on the product and the potential customer. Take time and research more. Take time and reflect on the research you did. Don't commission a research – that requires money. Become the researcher – that requires time.

At the same time there will be a tendency to flinch whenever you have to sign a cheque, because each cheque signed will tangibly deplete the reserves, even if it's just paying a phone bill. Every cheque you sign is for services rendered to you by another business – they did their job and you are paying them the fair value for it. This is exactly what you would wish for yourself in the business you are embarking on.

So smile when you sign a cheque as you would have someone sign you one very soon. Sign it from the heart and maybe even say thank you. Pay everyone a fair price because they will remember you paid them, even when you couldn't. Borrowing money comes with strings attached. Sometimes the strings are interest rates and other times it's worse – it's expectations and emotional baggage.

Avoid money that comes with emotional baggage – you have enough of your own already and it's only going to get heavier. Taking money from an uncle may seem convenient, but it will seem less convenient when he later demands that he sit in on a meeting, and play 'uncle.' Let uncles give you hugs and blessings.

If you are going to borrow money then borrow it in lieu of future services rendered, as a pre-pay for the future product. Make uncle a future customer, paying in advance at the best rate possible. You will then only owe him your product and not your soul. Don't take free money. No money is free. All money received has agenda. Feeling free of agenda, apart from your own is critical.

The seed capital lasted us well. We paid bills, ate judiciously, found joy in home food and saving electricity. We had no employees to pay and we hired teams on a part-time basis and paid them whatever we could with pre-agreed upon metrics for time spent. Theatre was largely amateur and therefore payment was perceived as a luxury. We could get away paying just the material suppliers and auditoriums and not having to pay the talent or the team. Because the truth was that we were offering them exposure and experience. But the catch is this, if you only offer them exposure and experience, then, in the future, someone will offer you just that and the inherent hypocrisy of the situation will not let you call the bluff on the deal.

We paid what we could. But we paid. When we paid people, it created a need to optimize our people needs because in the startup phase with the right PR, it's easy to attract a lot of young talent wanting to ride along, 'hang' and gain exposure. It's easy to take them on board because we feel like we could always use them somehow. But the minute you know their service is billable you pause, think and sieve through. You will find the best talent at the price you are offering.

Whenever we accepted the free talent offer we ended up losing them soon, after having trained them and gotten them task ready. The time we spent on them ended up being more expensive than actually paying them. We wasted a lot of time and a lot of talent and team used us. We spent lots of time on research. It turned out to be invaluable. Critics credited us later to have understood instinctively, what we actually researched heavily to find out. Research is that thing you do, when no one knows what you are doing, but only you know why. Research is a startup going undercover, to solve its own mysteries.

What we didn't have the appetite to do though, was to create products with our own money! We feared it would lead us into a deep hole of infinite time and investment, without knowing where it would stop. We hesitated to create, because we knew our reserves weren't enough to complete our creation. And what is completing? What defines completion? This uncertainty scared us. We doubted ourselves. This led us to become dependent on Toxic Funding. Toxic?

# Takeouts

- There is no set amount on what is enough startup capital. 'Enough' is a measure of inertia- the distance you put between yourself and getting started. Money is seldom the reason why businesses don't start – fear of money is. Define a number that you have the 'appetite to handle' and start the business from that level.

- Having more than enough money during your startup phase is not a blessing. Bootstrap yourself forcibly. Don't spend and hire expertise. Try and learn it hands on, and then later on hire the expertise you can manage.

- Use the time to build value, knowledge, training, efficiency etc., and that way you can convert the available time into money. Research a lot using the time available.

- Optimize your people needs because every person is a cost to the enterprise. In the entrepreneurship stage it's best to hire people who will do multiple things and not see themselves as a specialist in one activity alone.

- Pay people fairly and they will remember it. Don't try and get away with not paying them.

## Here is a simple exercise.

Define your living expenses, salaries to associates, rentals and all overheads, development costs, payments to suppliers, all for a period equivalent to the runway period. The sum total of all this, let's say, is X. Runway period is the period between the first day of the startup (on the accounts book) and the launch of product and first sale.

Now do the research, figure out the efficiencies achievable in developmental costs, package deals you could work out with suppliers with friendlier payment terms, best salary packages with a component linked to result post sale of product. Use the runway period to now decrease the X to a degree of at least 25%. Raise 1.5X as the startup capital. This way you will have a reserve of 0.75X (1.5X minus 0.75X) post-launch, and this will give you a further second runway period post-launch corrections, and running of the enterprise during this period.

## Chapter 5

# Toxic Funding

"What drives your bottom line primarily defines
who you are, or who you are becoming."

Year 1–5 was the greatest growth phase for Evam. Growth
in terms of the brand, awareness, first customers and first
word-of-mouth networks, and most importantly first
expectations, disappointments, learning and everything.

We generated record-breaking box office revenues
in our respective markets with our public productions
on stage, but also had record-breaking costs as well, since
we were one of the first entities defining ourselves as a
corporate and paying its talent and team resources.

We were funded by brands and sponsors who
were seeking commercial mileage by using us as an
unconventional media vehicle, in return for offering

them branding at the venue/in our content or tickets for premium customers. I call this funding instead of revenue because of the nature of the Return on Investments offered here. It made our bottom lines look good. It helped, in the short term. The money was working for us. However, it didn't take long for that 'placebo' to act out.

An odd setback in the box office revenues and moderately escalating costs made the money from the sponsor become far more important than before and then suddenly the business looked lopsided. We had to start working for that money, instead of having it work for us. We had to start defining sponsor deliverables as primary, and all else became less important, or at least equally important.

Meetings with sponsors and brands became more critical and we developed an entire culture that began to knock on and woo brands into working with us. We realized we were going the media way. We were no longer content, we were media. What drives your bottom line primarily defines who you are or who you are becoming.

This was unviable. We were competing with other media, who were hungrier and more tuned to deliver cost per million viability for an advertiser. We were stressing ourselves out, and deflating our product's value. We were losing, however good the temporary numbers made it seem like growth.

## Toxic Funding...

This kind of funding keeps you dependent and doesn't release you from its grip. Your business model is unviable without it. It is funding and this cannot be confused with revenue. Revenue is the direct desired fallout of product delivery and therefore an item that the business can, on an ongoing basis, become more poised towards delivering more value for.

Items such as sponsorship are ancillary revenues that accrue from product delivery and the product/solution and business model will become very different if the business were to re-align to attract more of this revenue. There can be different kinds of toxic funding. An investor whose agenda is more important than the agenda and vision of your business, will be slightly more antsy than your business can afford. It'll make you question whether your business' purpose is to realize its potential or to create returns that realizes the investors' estimation of its potential. Every quarter could become a discussion on measurement instead of gauging direction.

And there is the placebo funding. A source of revenue, funding or cost rationalizing that seems to bolster the bottom line and fatten it up to a healthy roundness but when it is removed the business may not seem so worthy or bang for buck. There will be many fallout revenues/funding that will come along with your business that needs to be seen as 'additional,' rather than 'core.' Ask yourself, 'Does the business model hold without it?' Be objective about what the core revenue to the product/solution delivery is and what the ancillary is. Make aggressive plans to drive the core revenues and always make sure ancillary revenues are attracted, but not depended upon.

This objectivity is critical in defining what you are driving the future of your business towards. What you call core will determine what the future holds for you. Everything can't be core, and if you treat everything as core, then nothing is core. Be unemotional about what you define as the business model. Be objective. The business model is that model of revenue and cost which when taken into account, will allow for a quiet smooth machine to function on its own, profitably. This functioning is independent of ancillary revenue streams, which should only add to the core functioning.

If ancillaries grow over time and become more solid and predictable, then float them off into a separate business model, which would mean this is a partner project to the core product.

Year 6 onwards we strove to find an independent box office model without sponsors, and also ventured into other content-based products beyond theatre. How that panned out we will read about later, but it removed us from the pressure of a path that was taking us away from the product and its relation to the customer. It was path changing for us and that was much needed, owing to our over-dependence on something toxic. Not toxic intrinsically, but toxic for us.

We let go of something that constituted 30% of our revenues. People thought we were being crazy. Everybody had an opinion. We knew we would have to work harder to create something even more valuable that replaced that amount. People saw it as loss of glory, and we saw it as a quest for sustainability. People thought we would spiral into a nightmare. The truth was we knew we would have to work harder, but also, for the first time, we slept better.

What brings an entrepreneur good sleep, though?

# Takeouts

- What drives your bottom line primarily defines who you are, or who you are becoming.

- Toxic funding is that ancillary funding that makes the entire value creation cycle unviable, when it gets removed. There are different forms of this – an investor with a side agenda beyond the core business, placebo funding etc.

## Here is an exercise.

Name all your revenue streams and cost efficiencies. Cost efficiencies such as an able supplier who gives you goods/ services at lesser than market rate etc., must be counted as revenue, since the reason why the supplier is extending you this favor could change with time and season and then you will suddenly find your margins disappearing.

Now figure which revenues/cost efficiencies are directly linked to the product doing well in the market – those that have a direct impact on the stock/product moved off the shelf or services sold! These are the non-toxic sustainable sources of funding and therefore real revenue options. Put them down and build a business that is driven by that bottom line.

Chapter 6

# Conscience

"Every entrepreneur seeks to be a part of the
solution and sometimes we end up becoming a part
of the problem."

Sleep...

All entrepreneurship is answering an inner calling.
Beyond the need to make a living, provide for yourself, do
something productive with one's life. There is something
deep in us that makes us wake up, want to change the world
and become the solution, so to speak.

Gandhiji said, 'Be the change you want to see in the
world,' and Michael Jackson sang, 'I'm starting with the
Man in the mirror.' Entrepreneurship is the embodiment
of this spirit. Where we seek to become the solution that
we want to see, and the therefore the first, and sometimes

the last customer, is the Man in the Mirror. So I assure you, beyond the challenges of daily work and market, internal communication and chaos, bottom line and overheads, there is something else altogether that will determine whether you sleep well or not.

I feel mildly intimidated to drop the word now, and I know I'm stirring up something that may be much more than this book can handle – but let me dare to, in the spirit of starting up – the word is 'conscience.' What is conscience?

It is answering that man in the mirror truthfully and straight – looking into his eyes and communicating. Is the product/solution matching the need it addresses?

Is it the best you could do, given the resources and constraints and knowing that resources are always limited and that constraints are always unlimited?

Would you be happy to receive it as a service/solution?

Is it priced fairly, doing justice to the effort and is it meaningful in terms of value to the customer?

Is there something you haven't shared with someone – your customer or your colleagues – that is making you restless?

Do you think the product is good, or only good enough? Are you working further on turning good enough into good?

Is the money you are raising/spending/making clean according to you?

Are you willingly listening to customer feedback or are you busy reacting to it and defending your actions?

And here is the toughest one- Are you listening to the things that your team is thinking but are finding difficult to say to you? Or are you busy barking instructions to them and keeping them busy?

Every entrepreneur seeks to be a part of the solution and sometimes we end up becoming a part of the problem.

Our rational minds and left brain can easily function with operational efficiencies, positive bottom lines and even be okay with 'being a part of the problem,' if the results are bearable. But the right brain and the emotional self does not function well if there is a void at the center of it all.

## What will bring you sleep then?

Knowing that you are on the path that feels right to you – not just the right path as prescribed by investors, market or even me and this damn book. Right by you! And great sleep is the most worthy thing to earn. That is your inner bottom line. That is your conscience.

Chapter 7

# Founders

"The people who come up with the idea, are the most key - the core group of people who dream the idea and commit to its realization."

It's easy to quantify the beginning of an entrepreneurship – the year it was founded, seed capital, the test phase, the launch of product, sales, top lines, bottom lines and everything else.

But even more significant than the day the idea behind Evam was born, or even Evam was born, was the day I met the person who became the co-founder of Evam, my classmate, friend and comrade, Sunil Vishnu K.

He was just like me in a few ways – he didn't have entrepreneurship in his blood; both of us got into marketing school with a passion for Theatre; both of us didn't ever consider entrepreneurship as an option; we were looking for means to finding a living and were getting ready for the rat race; both knew deep down that we could run the rat race well, if we chose to, but also that we would tire easily if we did; we didn't have rich parents, but surely had understanding (or at least highly tolerant) ones.

Sunil was from Bhopal, and I was from Madras, neither city was known for its entrepreneurial culture, nor were they cultural hubs of professional theatre practices. We vibed well and had mutual regard and respect for each other's qualities. We didn't know what the future held for us, but our instinct did tell us that if we stuck together, the future would seem less daunting to dream about. Dreaming can be scary, especially when done alone. You may end up thinking you are a madman, or the very least, a greedy one.

## The Avengers

This was coming. The minute I used Bruce Wayne as a reference to make a point, I knew I had to appease the MCU (Marvel Comic Universe) and its bhakts. So here is my token appeasement to set the world back in order. Every idea is deemed with its own destiny when it is founded. This destiny has a lot of factors affecting it, many factors beyond its control and a few critical ones within its control. The product idea and its timing are some key obvious controllable ones.

But the people who come up with the idea, are the most key – the core group of people who dream the idea and commit to its realization. The strength, resilience and mettle of these people are what will be tested in the journey of the idea to its fruition. A mediocre idea like human beings saving the earth becomes a lot more exciting and (ironically) believable when we describe the Avengers and each of their particular strengths. We can be rest assured that New York may get destroyed but the rest of the world will be saved.

Pick a partner/team that has complementary strengths. It is easy to get attached to like-minded people, but be aware and resist this while forming the core group for your startup. Like-minded bonding is great for a friendship or something closer, but for an idea to be realized it requires people with different strengths and weaknesses.

Weaknesses of one should ideally be mitigated by the strengths of another.

What could bring together all these dissimilar people is the commonality of the cause. The vision of the idea/solution/organization becomes this commonality of purpose that bonds the founding fathers (or mothers!). If this sounds very similar to the birth of a nation, I would not discourage it from being seen that way.

An entrepreneurship is a little nation with its own purpose, culture, economy, social hierarchies and even holy cows. Pick people for the core group that you instinctively trust – this is everything in the lifetime of an idea. The stronger the instinct to trust the other, the richer the DNA of its genesis. The trust the founders of the organization show in each other is the trust the entire organization will exhibit. This trust is exhibited by the founders in the way they discuss an idea, however combative the points of view may be, there will be no fear and miscommunication when there is trust. All ideas will be debated openly and truthfully and this is the culture that will pervade in the organization top down.

Later on in an organizations' life when there are disputes in IP, valuations or moneys, people often blame greed for having created this divisiveness in trust. Usually this mistrust begins much earlier on, in the founding period of the idea. Money is merely a symptom of this mistrust growing and taking tangible form.

If you don't trust someone in the core group, address that mistrust or better still, change the core group, however strong that person's contribution is likely to be. Generally, people with a desire to be an entrepreneur tend to be quiet and uncommunicative, about this desire, sometimes even with themselves. They tend to hold their cards to their chest. So when you do meet someone you feel like sharing these ideas with, allowing you to let go of that sense of caution, it's usually a good sign.

There have been many points of time in the Evam journey, where having a comrade in the journey has actually felt like additional pressure because in a way both our fortunes and efforts had become inextricably linked to the fate of Evam. Which means, if on a bad day, during a bad phase, I felt like waking up and running away from it all but couldn't because I was answerable to at least one other person. But a commitment to the common cause helped both of us through our bad phases. We each had our cycles of energy and positivity and therefore it was a ship with two captains who could each take command depending on who was feeling stronger and well rested.

Although we came from similar backgrounds, the differences in our personalities helped Evam. Sunil is patient, social, approachable and open to new ideas. I am less of all these things. I am confident, innovative, big thinking and optimistic. Sunil is less of all these things.

Most people who have worked with Evam, the brand, have liked the combination of us. We work well together. And we have enjoyed working together. That's mostly the journey of Evam – enjoying the working together.

# Takeouts

- Pick a partner/team that has complementary strengths. Always think 'Avengers!'

- Pick people in the core group that you trust, or make sure you build trust with. If there is any iota of mistrust or gaping gaps in communication, then that will only give way sooner or later and eventually blow over.

- Communicate with each other and within the core group and make all confrontation also communication. The trust you exhibit with each other is the trust that the people in organization will place in each other.

## Here is a compatibility exercise.

Debate on a point that you and your core group member/s or co-founders are in disagreement with, the more basic the disagreement and deeper the beliefs and the clashes in viewpoints, the better. Some difficult topics could be religion, origins, identity or views on ethics. Debate it to its end and see how violent the communication gets. I don't believe that you should get into fisticuffs but you should push each other mentally for the sake of the debate and see how you handle the conflict. Keeping respect and decorum and trust within this conflict will tell you how you will handle crisis, money and intellectual property later. It's okay to disagree but how the disagreement is communicated will tell you everything about the future.

## Chapter 8

# Human Resources

"No participant is a waste of time."

The first people who came on aboard Evam became very important to us.

Our first colleagues/employees/associates. All these words we devised later, but initially they all felt like family who had found us. That bunch of people became blood-related to us as if the enterprise was the family and they completed the picture.

They worked harder, came in earlier, stayed longer and were hungry with us.

Preethi was our first colleague. Our junior, from when we were in MICA. She held a good job that she nabbed off campus and was sitting pretty with a cushy corporate life. When she heard about us venturing into Evam, a realization of a dream that started at college, she was immediately excited and she offered to join us. The offer seemed unbelievable – a young intelligent post graduate joining a garage startup with an un-established business model and a dream of making a living from arts and its management. We were touched by the show of faith.

We offered her equal executive partnership, not ownership, but a guarantee that she would draw as earnings, whatever the founders earned for themselves. It was the best assurance we could give for this leap of faith she took with us.

Preethi gave us her best in those startup years. For me, personally, she became the glue that kept the enterprise together. Her presence ensured that I could venture into slightly more imaginative strategic thinking for the future with the assurance that today will be handled ably. She was with us for three years. The three critical years. But 3 years hence it was time for her to move on. After having given Evam the three best years of her and its life! I suddenly felt like an arm was threatening to get severed from the being. I didn't act dramatically or react emotionally, I did the usual thing that most self-respecting entrepreneurs do, we clam up when we feel slighted.

The parting was outwardly cordial, but I felt everything about it to be unreasonable. Had we not been fair? Had we not done our best for her? Wasn't she supposed to stay for the long haul and become an owner, a business head? What could be more compelling in her life than this? What was so compelling that it had to be done with us out of the equation? I felt slighted and angry about this departure. Like a breakup was being forced upon us.

## Who are these people in the building?

An entrepreneur seldom measures the time they spend on the entrepreneurship. We lose track of the time and energy we spend in maintaining the mission, let alone accomplishing it. We don't eat well, fitness jumps out of the window and a social life is only what the movies and media lead us to believe people have. Even the breaks we take are mildly abusive on our health, but gather us a breath maybe (my choice of poison during breaks was coffee).

But all around us are people 'in the building' who seem to be equally captivated by our mission and seem to be discussing things and debating with us heatedly, passionately, on plenty. These are team members, senior mentors, good-intentioned friends, and colleagues. They came in once the mission was put into place and its often perplexing for the entrepreneur to understand why they seem so taken with this – 'this' something that was born out of a strange dream you had some odd day and felt that the picture on the wall should not be tilted. At the least, this dream has been an extravagance of yours.

It can be overwhelming to see so many people in the building who are behaving like they care too. It fills you with gratitude, and like all good things that we initially feel thankful for, it eventually numbs us into rationalizing this as normal – only because it's overwhelming to remain in a high state of gratitude all the time. And whenever we rationalize something as normal, we tend to normalize it as rational! Hence we start learning to see this interaction as transactional. 'Hey, they get something out of it I'm sure, and therefore I can continue assuming that this is natural and will remain!'

This leads to what I call the wrath of disloyalty, where every person who leaves the journey of the entrepreneurship will be seen by the founders as having given up the cause and gone astray! They will be seen as disloyal, ungrateful and dramatic doors will be closed. This is totally uncalled for.

Your cause is worthy, surely to you, and it's the mission of the enterprise to make it worth something to the world eventually. To others, this cause is worth a contribution, but only a contribution. They will come into the journey and participate – in this process they will learn and even 'waste your time.' But no participant is a waste of time. Every moment spent educating a colleague or an associate is your learning that you are on the path and someday in the future they will tell someone else this story as an urban legend, if you treat them with dignity.

Every colleague, mentor and sometimes co-founder is a part of the journey and they are meant to give something to the journey. It's good to feel grateful for taking this and also feel selfish for keeping it. It was meant to be shared for the brand. They won't stay and it's ridiculous to expect them to or hold them to it. If you don't shut doors after them, they will proudly talk of this association and make more meaning of the brand. The dignity, with which you let them go, is the investment you make to have them speak of you positively in the future, to the society at large.

The building will always be full, but will and almost should always be full with mostly different people and new connections. Contributions will be vital and nothing will be a 'waste of time,' although it will seem like it a lot!

Preethi left us and the parting was very cordial. Years later I realize what a self-centered naive reaction that was because since then that colleague and friend has remained the greatest objective mirror for Evam. But that was in spite of the passive wrath I showed her when she left. Evam wouldn't be what it is today without the contributions of so many people- part time, full time, no time and all time. Every journey counts and they all funnel in and add to the brand it is. Those people in the building are the building and what it stands on.

# Takeouts

- Take responsibility for your organization and the people in it – they will pass on that sense of responsibility to your brand and their work. At the same time, just because you have a sense of responsibility towards them it doesn't make them answerable to you personally. It is a professional relationship and all expectations must stay within that ambit.

- Treat people with dignity and also those who are leaving. Because they can then become positive spokespeople for the organization and for the brand.

- People leaving the organization is natural and inevitable. Don't subject them to your wrath – instead appreciate them for their contribution and give them the opportunity to work with you in a different capacity at a later time.

- And like I said in an earlier chapter – pay people fairly, and don't try and not pay them when you can. A missed paycheque or an unfair pay package will be interpreted as disrespect and will lead to mistrust.

Chapter 9

# Culture

"Culture is what the people do even when no one is watching, especially when no one is watching."

Ours was an entertainment company in its founding definition, Evam 'Entertainment.' We entertained through live stage performances and wooed audiences into getting themselves some entertainment on weekends. A lot of our actual work was therefore in auditoriums, promotions of the events were at malls and hangouts, and mostly over Saturdays and Sundays. When everyone was enjoying their leisure, we were working hard, delivering our entertainment as their leisure.

This made work hours at Evam very strange. We had to encourage people to come in late, because we knew we would be making them stay late, since rehearsals with amateur actors (only we ourselves were professional actors, since we had quit to do this full time) started post their office hours and went on very late. We would also be eating into their weekends and when the rest of the world was sulking on a Monday morning, my team would have just hit the bed after a late late Sunday-night wrap-up.

We worked with a lot of young people so the energy of the organization was automatically young, and since we were aiming to appeal to young people, we became more youthful. Like-minded people were attracted to the movement therefore work always felt like a bunch of familiar friends hanging out. Cliques started forming, and hangouts were planned. Hanging out happened at strange times because work hours could never be clearly defined. Work hours changed according to our work, and there was always enough work.

The world of amateur theatre and drama had its own peculiar practices and we didn't know whether we had to follow them or not. For instance, at the end of each set of shows an amateur theatre group will throw itself a cast party, a party where the cast and crew celebrate the weekend of shows and make merry. We never felt the need for this because we had shows lined up almost every other week and this would feel like throwing a party at the end of every workday.

Such decisions where people's time, energy and practices were to be decided were truly tough decisions because they all affected, positively or negatively, the employee morale, and eventually their productivity and energy.

We suddenly felt like our college faculty, imposing rules and restrictions. We felt we should do better than they used to. After all, school and college days were behind us and this should not feel like a hard-nosed corporate company either! We made many mistakes with these decisions.

## The air in the room...

There is a single word that defines all the things mentioned in the previous page. When all the employees leave office and work is still ticking away in your head. Everything seems quiet and empty, that emptiness is still filled with an invisible air and that is called culture. Culture is how an organization looks at time, space and energy.

How does the 'little nation' look at how it spends its time? Therefore, what value do they place on the customer's time? How does its people treat the space that they work in and also spaces that they go to for work – be it a client's office, a mall where a bunch of team members are merely hanging out while they're on duty or even something as basic as civic sense of the people in the team? What is the nature, tone of the actions of the team and what does each action say to each other, to the customer, to the client, to the world....

In that sense, what does the organization stand for? All this is culture. It defines the nature that the organization encourages in its people. Culture is what the people do even when no one is watching, especially when no one is watching. For an entrepreneur, the best thing about culture is that it can be defined and set. Once it's defined and set, it acts like the rivets that hold the entire machinery together, invisibly and securely.

But the not-so-great thing about culture is that when everything is culture how do you set it without seeming like your college management board that came up with random rules and ID cards and therefore never got taken seriously. How do you set culture without seeming like you are setting it?

And the worst thing about culture is that once set, it can't be un-set! It's very difficult to change the way we do things or the way things get done, once they settle in. The product can change, the solution can change and the marketing variables can change. Culture unfortunately changes at the speed of biological evolution.

I have a fabulous suggestion on how to set culture. It's fabulous because I think it is and also it's a hit-nerve-center approach.

Money is the most critical thing in any startup in the startup phase. It is the most revered entity whether it's incoming or outgoing money. It is often spoken about in hushed tones and its presence generates a sense of assurance, while its absence creates a sense of quiet anxiety and hope. It is that thing we talk least about, and yet worry most about. Set your culture from the point of view of how you treat 'Money.'

- How do you set value for a product? How do you negotiate value and enable your team to fix price?

- How do you let team handle cash and report back with accountability?

- How do you treat a loss-making project? How do you handle the disappointment?

- How do you treat surplus and profits? Do you let it overwhelm you, and how do you share it with the team, both the news and the booty?

- How do you link time to money, space to money and energy spent to money?

It's easy to be strict about time, energy and space, and then have completely different values about money but this sends out mixed signals to your nation. According to someone with a middle-class mindset, if you treat money with a sense of justice, where none of your rules are too strict, or too lax, then your diktats about time, space and energy will be respected and taken seriously. Start with how you treat money and then extend that to all other practices in the organization. You will be seen walking the talk rather than making an arbitrary management rule....

As founders, playing culture police was difficult. Whenever we deployed a cultural practice at Evam or a must/should do, there were quiet murmurs and immediate acceptance seldom happened. That never felt good. We felt like bad cops. We hated being seen that way. We wished we could bend the rules and play good cops. This was never helpful in the long run. Worse was when we hardened and stood our ground, like bad cops becoming badass cops. This alienated the people around us and made us seem like authority figures. This hurt in the short term itself. Culture is meant to be pondered and chosen. Choose the right path for yourself. This comes from the kind of atmosphere you wish to create in your nation. What you celebrate and create a sense of value for is what will be celebrated.

We enforced some practices and organically let other practices change with time – a combination of rules where things were non-negotiable and leeway where people could decide things for themselves. Not everything was democratic. Some things were democratic and that process was surely enjoyable. But the most critical things were not. They were things we decided to hold sacred and made a big deal about and even a policy for.

# Takeouts

- Culture can be defined and set. This is the best thing to know because once set it just needs to monitored.

- Even if you don't set one, a culture will develop on its own. Therefore you might as well create a culture, a set of beliefs and practices that exemplify those beliefs – that is desirable for the organization.

Chapter 10

# Investor Need

"When things are tough borrow debt, not equity."

End of Year 5. It was our first presentation to an investor. We were truly growing out of the infancy phase! The choice of investor was ours. It was an ideal fit. A performing arts management entrepreneurship seeking equity from a leading multiplex entertainment brand based out of Chennai. We were genuinely excited to part with equity with such a respected and relevant brand and have them participate in the Evam journey.

The fund flow situation was grave and the truth was we needed the fund boost badly, and therefore the equity participation from the right partner seemed like a good fit. We were sinking due to a few failed projects, our monthly overheads were stretching us to the max and we had still not cracked a sustainable stable business model. We had a lot of hopes pinned onto this meeting. We had sent in our valuations and expectations and we were confident about getting ourselves a good deal. After all, the investor was someone we looked up to and he would certainly do what's best for us.

We got into the room and he invited us with warmth and a positive smile. That was a good sign. We were on the verge of a yes, and a way forward. I felt reassured and relaxed. He sat us down and said yes! Score! He told us he would have to tweak the valuations slightly to make it better and we agreed that that would be fair. He assured us that he would do his best to make sense of the situation. We nodded in gleeful resonance. After the butterflies were calmed, and an air of assurance was established, he looked at us and said, 'Don't do it!'

## Investment need...

When is the best time to accommodate an investor? *When you don't need it...* Sounds ironic and even counter-intuitive?

Because when you actually need it is when you are emotionally blinded by what all the funding could be used for. All signs will point to Rome not because of logic or instinct, but because of desperate need. And the dangerous truth about monetary needs is that all desperate monetary needing situations are quicksands.

Financial quicksands are those ideas, projects or situations that consume far greater liquidity than anticipated, and appear as if they're solving problems by throwing more money into it. That's the mirage of the quicksand. The nature of the quicksand is that it's a vortex, and one that wisdom, rather than wealth, has to solve!

An investor takes equity. Equity is ownership. And when the need is highest, the valuation of the company will be at its most vulnerable. The new (part) owner could set down terms that look absurd once the haze of the financial need has been lifted. So please take my word for it, when the need is highest, objectivity and clear-headed judgment will be hard to find. Emotions will run high and when that is the case, don't sell!

When is the best time to accommodate an investor then? When everything is stable and the numbers look good, and there is no apparent need for anything, except maybe taking things to the next level. This would mean that a stable foundation has been laid for a profitable revenue stream and the culture (not necessarily the market) is well entrenched to keep this momentum going. This would mean that the value of the foundation is apparent to both the investor and you, without over emphasizing on the toil and the blood and sweat that has gone into it.

We should never have to overemphasize the blood we shed and the toil you underwent in order to gain a better valuation. That is but the icing on the cake, for that the cake has to be the business and its functions.

So what does one do when the need is high? Sit down and do the small yet effective things – cost cutting, increasing product value to customer, downsizing, and investing, if not money, atleast energy and time into future solutions because the market will turn, and so will your fortunes, and one needs to be ready when that turn comes. And borrow debt, not equity.

A half hour later we were walking out without a deal – I was not sure whether we were to interpret the analysis of us as positive or negative. Did this mean he actually didn't want stake in Evam? Was this his way of gently rejecting the offer? I was angry and confused. Which means I was emotional and chaotic. I did not fully understand what happened and what he meant. My ego was bruised, which is always a sure shot sign of miscommunication.

We went back to the drawing board on many things. We let go of employees, with remorse and a heavy heart, we wrote off our own salaries, and we reanalyzed future projects through a scanner of returns to investments ratios. And I can't tell you how manically we went about all this. Because we knew we didn't have an option.

Results of all this showed a year or so later. But it gave us self-belief and made us resilient.

Today, I realize the value of his 'Don't do it!' Doing it then would have meant selling out when the valuation was the lowest. We would have diverted all that funding into financial quicksands. We would not have innovated or been forced into changing the way we operated. Because the way we were operating was what got us into that situation in the first place.

I now realize that the investor was a friend first. He proved he was a mentor to us and assured us that we could have whatever we wanted, but made us realize what we actually needed. We needed to course correct. We earned resilience and self-confidence in the process.

# Takeouts

- Don't go to an investor when you badly need money. You will not know your value, and the desperation of the situation will lead to compromises on your value.

- Beware of financial quicksands into which you intend to throw the funds from the investments. They could make the funds quickly disappear and then leave you where you started, now that you have given up equity. Use wisdom to solve the issue rather than wealth.

- Go to an investor when the business is stable, performing well and has a clear demonstrable business model. In this case, the investor's money and advice would be strategically valuable to take things to the next level, rather than solve ailing current issues. It puts you on a good footing to be taken seriously.

- When things are tough borrow debt, not equity.

# Quality: Self Startup

The difference between following an agenda set for you and achieving success based on pre-defined criteria, and having to set your own agenda and understanding the success and failure from your own definitions is like the difference between the earth and sky. All our lives we have had agendas set for us. We have known when we were supposed to move up from kindergarten to junior school, and then from school to college, etc. In the middle of all this we have exams and their cyclical nature that define activities and goals across the year. We constantly know how we are doing, because the results indicate our progress and we are told how we can do better!

We know when to get married, and when it's acceptable to have children. We know what the median earning in our peer group is and there is great comfort in staying within these reference points. It's a pre-decided life with pre-defined leeway and you play freely, but within this range. Have fun, do whatever you want, but stay within the box, which has several small boxes within it. Ticking all these boxes and staying within them is reassuring.

Entrepreneurship, especially in the startup phase is letting go of all of this! Becoming your own boss makes you the master of time, energy, money, (a significant part of) your destiny and also how you interpret it. You define what to work on. You define the results expected. You then define how, when, how much, whom to do it for/with, when you set the alarm to wake up, what to wear and even when to ring the bell and call it a day. This is like starting a school, setting the syllabus, making a big deal of exams outcomes, conducting the exam, correcting the papers and then rewarding the winners and admonishing those who didn't, except you're both, the student and the teacher.

Anarchy is what would be unleashed if you suddenly gave someone who has never experienced freedom, infinite amounts of it. A startup is a constant rebellion, not allowing this potential anarchy from happening. It is setting rigours, checks and balances, culture, rewards and reviews to ensure the world you have created has order and answerability.

## Ask yourself this

- How much of a self-starter are you?

- How good are you at learning something new, without anyone blatantly telling you how you are doing?

- How good are you at setting forth and achieving something without social validation pouring in?

- How good are you at slow, excruciating incremental progress, much like an ant building a home?

- How do you handle someone mocking what you are doing and its futility?

- How do you handle failing repeatedly and not having the option of giving up?

- How flexible are you in the face of adversity?

## Here are some simple experiments

- Did you ever have a pet? How hands-on and responsible a pet owner were you? This will give you a measure of your ability to handle responsibility concertedly

- Did you ever learn a skill for which no one sent you to do a course in? Did you enjoy it and did you learn more? This will help you evaluate yourself as a self-learner and understand the rigour with which you approach something that you don't have anyone else monitoring.

- Have you failed at something, have people laugh at you, still manage to have fun doing it and kept at it, until you got better and maybe even mildly good? This will give you a measure of the need for social validation versus personal curiosity and satisfaction – your internal barometer of worth.

- Did you ever do something where you didn't cheat or didn't have to? This is your ability to report to yourself!

- Self-starter, are you? How long do you plan to take to finish this book, and can you achieve it in that time?

# Act II

# Quality: Control

In the 'infant' startup phase an entrepreneur is going to enjoy the responsibility of making decisions. Moving from a space in life where we are at the receiving end of instructions and others' decisions, entrepreneurship offers us the release of having our decisions take form and become something real! It gives us an outlet for our 'instincts' and 'ideas.' The rest of the organization will get an opportunity to see you as the leader and this is a very simple mode of taking instructions. People know where the power lies and start getting used to understanding the nature of the organization from its actions and decisions.

It is in this phase where this format of leadership works best and it is much needed in order to instill the DNA of the founders into the nature of the organization.

But once you're in the 'adolescent' startup phase it is this very instinct and power that could inhibit the organization and stop its organic growth. If people just followed instructions, then the following two things will happen. One, the strong-headed 'ideas' people may leave the organization if they feel unheard and only the instruction takers will remain. Two, the organization will come to a standstill until the employees are given instructions by the senior leadership and in the case of crisis situations, this is tantamount to awaiting instructions to call fire service, during a fire, while you've been standing next to a fire extinguisher the whole time!

This phase is where the entrepreneur has to create instruction and feedback mechanisms that are people and systems driven, rather than doing it all autocratically. Empowering people to take ownership and defining scopes within which they can make their own decisions should become the norm. These decisions, within the scope, should not be questioned too many times before they yield results. As much as these decisions could go wrong, it creates a culture of taking ownership and feeling responsible. The best team is the one with one leader, but everyone in it should be capable of stepping it up and leading when their moment arrives. Also this is the first symptom of sustainability- can the organization function without the active participation and interference of the core team and how smooth would that functioning be. Revenue models may indicate sustainability but this sustainable culture will only ensure its continuous achievement. Making yourself unnecessary is critical for the growth of your startup. You must be sought for the new visioning and exploring of unfamiliar avenues but routine decisions and daily operations cannot need you.

At the same time learn to *demarcate your skill and the role of leadership.* Most startup founders are very skilled at the craft of the business. Coding specialists in a tech startup, engineering whiz' in a product startup, consumer behavior specialists in a B2C startup, etc. But it's important to realize that you learn to distinguish this from your responsibilities as a leader. If it's your startup, then you are probably the leader! In which case you are a leader first and a skilled professional next. If you get too busy showing off your skill, then that's not only a poor use of your time, but it also becomes the benchmark for skill within the organization. If you have to lead, then simply use your knowledge of skill *to* hire more skilled associates. This will take some overcoming of your ego. Overcome it. You anyway have more power as leader so you might as well take on that role for the predominant portion of the time.

M S Dhoni is more valuable to India as the captain of the cricket team, than just as a batsman in the lineup. And the control that you enjoyed in the 'infant' phase? Let go of it. Control things with systems and through people. Let go of that remote control and puppet strings. Teach your people how to fish and stop fishing, and welcome to the 'adolescent phase!'

Chapter 11

# Decision Making

**"A deep-seated conviction of how things will turn out or should turn out – this is called instinct."**

I love the act of using the *Lego* blocks of data and building my own sculptures of information. I grab data and I try to look at it from all perspectives, and then discuss it with my team. But all the while I know there is a deep-seated conviction of how things will turn out or should turn out – this is called instinct. It resides inside of you and sometimes never leaves the building. It may rot, it may become lazy, but it won't leave. I play devil's advocate with the data and try and reason with that instinct, like a lawyer presenting his case before a judge, and also acknowledging the instinct, who is the defense counsel. I try and beat every argument for its worth and then let the judge decide. And more often than not that judge is emotional. Unless he hears rational enough arguments, he is going to act like an emotional being, do something grand and maybe even silly.

I have already told you about our postgraduate thesis and the results of the study with respect to what it indicated to us - it said, 'Don't Startup!' And yet we did. Even later we have disregarded data and information and gone into many projects, backing our instinct. Has it always paid off? No. I wish I could say yes and make an impassioned plea that inspires the human spirit. But no, it hasn't always paid off.

## Instinct and Information

At every point of time we are making decisions and even when we don't answer a call or reply to an email, a decision is being made. Most of these decisions are made based on information, situations, feasibility and instinct. The instinct that an entrepreneur has is often talked about and even poetry gets written about the genius behind key decisions made and how they were dictated by instinct.

Instinct is something intrinsic in us. It is some barometer inside that gives us a sense of what could go right or wrong and even act like a predictor of how things could play out based on the decisions we make. It's the part that detectives use to solve murder mysteries and great scientists use to say, 'Eureka,' when they invent something that has not existed until now.

Instinct is fabulous, but only until things go wrong. When things fall and the analyses are conducted we have no basis for having made the decision except for someone's instinct. When the person is asked why they chose what they chose, no amount of rationalizing will make sense of it when you compare it with the results that one knows the decision to have turned out to be.

Entrepreneurs with instinctive successes have many odes written to them but instinctive failures are called losers. Because beyond the romance and mystery behind instinct, sometimes it is basically *laziness masquerading as sixth sense.*

We don't know, and worse still, we don't bother to find out, and worst of all we haven't bothered to find out. We don't consider knowledge or results, and yet we stick to a perspective or point of view that our mind projects that it is convinced about. Most often instinct is this sloth.

However, when you have all information, have commissioned all the studies, gotten the tips from the locals, seen the weather conditions ahead of you and yet you believe that you ought to set sail, then that is compelling instinct. Because you will now regard everybody's speculation with a little more respect and create a plan that will account for all fortifications needed for the course ahead. If your instinct says you should fly then you should, but not without wings and checking the draft of wind.

Instinct backed with information is the essence of *James Bond*, *Sherlock Holmes* and every Eureka moment. Without information and effort, all instinct is idle judgment, preconception, mere hope and hubris!

So here is the way to maneuver instinct and information at every decision-making point. An EQ flowchart so to speak-

First gather all the relevant information. Everything is information – someone else's opinion, people's perceptions, actual data, past events and trends, future predictions done by market, even other team members' opinions – everything that you can't find in your gut!

Glean all that you can glean from this information and create a strong case for the devil's advocate.

Next put down, before going into the decision debate, what your instincts are telling you with respect to this decision. When I say put down, I don't mean write down, – don't do that. Make what your instincts are saying clear to yourself so that when the information is presented to you, you will notice those instincts organically change or become more steadfast. Either way you should know what your instinct is telling you before getting into to the process.

Later on you will realize why your instinct said what it said to you. This realization is invaluable to knowing yourself.

Now, debate. Debate for hours with the core team. Then stop all the debate when you have heard enough, or when everybody has had a say.

If the information has overwhelmed the instinct, then it's an easy decision to make. It means that your instinct listened to the information and has allowed itself to change.

If the information did not change your instinct, then here is my advice, go with your instinct.

This is dangerous advice, but I'll tell you why.

If the instinct prevailed over information, then go with it. This is not to say that your instinct is right. It may not be. But it means that you are convinced about a certain approach that may seem counter-logic, and yet you are willing to put all your effort into this approach.

This approach may or may not solve the problem at hand. If it does, good.

It may not, but yet it will teach you something – it will end up trying something that no logical approach would have even attempted and something entirely new will come out of it. This is usually how 'Disruptive Invention' is achieved.

Backing your instinct usually means you are willing to put in the effort, use your intelligence and resources into an attempt, and all such effort yields something. It may not solve the problem at hand, but it will lead to new learnings for sure. And when you back your instinct, you end up working doubly hard to prove yourself and this usually helps in any project. It brings out the deepest commitment in you and that's always a good thing. This is your ego being put to positive work.

Evam itself was a product of this instinct. Maybe we didn't solve what we set out to do but we found an entirely new way in the process. Having said that, information is wealth and it needs to always be respected. Respect makes sure we fetch the information, process it and consider it deeply and allow our instincts to be influenced by it.

# Takeouts

- The very instinct of entrepreneurship could be an emotional choice, but all decisions within it should not be. It's important to follow through with a combination of emotion and reason. Humans are essentially emotional beings. Channel that emotion into following through on a decision made and remove it from the decision-making process itself. Don't rely on instinct alone.

- Follow the EQ decision-making flowchart!

- Not having information is never a reason to rely on your instinct. Instinct becomes valuable only when it's an option – not when it's the only option.

## Chapter 12

# Products in the Market

"What you sell is not what the customer buys."

The most successful product of Evam in the first phase of our journey was the 'Plays.' We had resurrected the model of audiences buying tickets for a live performance. Buy tickets as much in advance as possible and consume the experience by appointment. This was a rare feat in an era where cinemas were becoming swanky multiplexes with plusher seats, better air conditioning, buttered up popcorn and buttered up everything else.

Cinemas are different from live performances since they have only notional rentals and operate on their own property. Live performances happen in hired venues, where the hiring happens by the hour. Cinemas have fixed overheads and make a killing when the show is full, and don't lose too much when it's not. Live performances depend heavily on the audience turnout on the day of show, because the next day or the previous day there may not be a show, or even ever again. It is a perishable item in the market scheme of things.

But the truth was this- a lot of plays were staged before, during and after we did them. Our plays could not have been that much better than the other offerings, keeping in mind that neither the founders nor the ecosystem we functioned in had any formal training in the arts. And yet we sold well and we were consumed with great satisfaction and by repeat audiences.

We were selling 'plays' or so we thought...

## What we sell and what is bought...

An entrepreneur obsesses about the product/solution so much so that they have subconsciously dreamt about it, consciously imagined it, sensed it forming given it a structure and rolled out the carpet for its full release. Entrepreneurs are well aware and believe they need to have a complete hold over this aspect of the business. And this is how it ought to be – mildly obsessive and fully passionate.

But what happens when this product/solution leaves the enterprise to mingle with the market is what happens when a river merges into the ocean. In the delta region you can see the river and its distinct density, colour and nature, just as it merges into the deep blue of the ocean. After that one cannot make out the difference anymore. It's all ocean. What happens in this process is that the product/solution does not change but what it is being bought as, used for, talked about, and described to, by the customer changes.

Most often what an entrepreneur describes as a product/solution will be not be what the customer describes as having used or experienced. This is usually very stressful for the entrepreneur because while the entrepreneur is convinced that what they have is 'a newly formulated milk culture based coagulated slurry with a base of Carbohydrate in order to provide the body coolness, energy and also a probiotic lining to the stomach,' the customer will describe it as good ol' curd rice. This can be infuriating for the entrepreneur, who sees themselves as the parent of the product.

Most advertising is a desperate need to get the customer to say what the entrepreneur wants them to say. This is usually futile. A product/solution doesn't change the life of the customer as it does the life of the business. For the entrepreneur the product is life, whereas for the customer it's a small part of life and therefore they only need a code to refer to it. The way they see the product/ solution can be very humbling for the entrepreneur if the entrepreneur chooses to accept it as such.

*What you sell is not what the customer buys.* Once the river reaches the ocean, one should not try to separate the river from the ocean – that would be futile. It's important to understand how the river changes the nature of the ocean in a minuscule, yet discernible way. It wasn't the plays that were being bought as such. The product may have been the plays, but the brand was much more. It was the buzz, it was the 'like-minded' audiences who gathered together in a social atmosphere; it was the tone of the content of the plays and the overall flavour of positivity, hope, vibrancy and happiness! And here we thought it was good plays we were selling!

Once we knew what was actually being bought, we packaged that into our future products. We packaged the 'feeling.' One of those products became a division called 'Happy Factory.' The idea was simple- how to generate a good feeling of happiness at your workplace, by helping people come together and create something, using theatre as the base. We designed workshops and experiences for corporates. The product was not workshops; it was a feeling – mood transformation!

# Takeouts

- Once the product reaches the market, you need to see the market's perspective, much more than the maker's.

- Talk to the customer. Talk to the distributor. Talk to the critics. Those talks are the product – whether you like it or not. Humble that ego and become what is bought, rather than what is being sold. It takes empathy and listening with your heart and mind to get what the customer is saying.

- Be egoless in analyzing product reception. The lesser your ego interferes with this reception the greater will be the learning for version 2.0 and believe me all invention in an entrepreneurship is versioning. Things are always going to change, so they might as well get better, especially according to the customer.

- When you accept what the customer feels the product/ solution is, it gives you the clarity to not only innovate but to create new offerings based on how your brand is perceived. This is the difference between a product and a brand- a product is the solution to a problem that you are offering, a brand is the feeling that a customer is rewarded with (or punishment that a customer is subjected to) when they use your product. That's why brands are emotional while products are rational.

Chapter 13

# Success Hubris

"Every failure is a symptom of something that needs attention."

It was late 2009. Evam was 6 years old. We were getting national recognition. We had a successful product that was selling well, and a brand that was positioned uniquely and was well known, even though the truth was we didn't have our house in order yet entirely.

The successful product and its accompanying business delivery model were ready for a national rollout. It was ready, because that was the next logical step forward if the model was to be tested further. All local results seemed positive and the next logical step was national. This was the best time.

Were we confident about the model and the experiment that lay ahead? Yes, but only because we seemed to have positive mojo on our side and there was a general good feeling about product rollouts and the brand. No, because in our heart of hearts we knew the numbers were going to be pinned on hope for a considerable percentage of the project.

Hope *is the thing that should happen in order to make a project working well, work really well and become successful.* If this 'Hope' is an X Factor, which is a bunch of intangibles, and ifs and maybes, then the lifebuoy intended to keep you afloat could just be hope.

But 2009 was round the corner and we could have potentially ended that year having proven it all, and thereafter the world was going to be at our threshold. We chose a play based on a book that had national appeal. We acquired rights from the author and adapted it for stage. We had a produced a version of it earlier, and were familiar with its appeal and response. This was version 2.0 of a well-received product. Product positivity, check! We chose all the familiar markets, and also several new markets that we knew this book had a strong appeal in. Market positivity, check!

Our strongest core strength was ground marketing mojo and buzz, which is a highly valuable factor for the success of live events since it leads to ticket sales. We were strong in our local markets and we were looking to replicate that model in the new markets. Marketing positivity, check!

Funding was being sought after and a national sponsorship hunt was underway. 2009 was bad times market wise and spend on marketing wise, thanks to the USA imploding under the sub-prime crisis. Somehow, whatever happens in USA seems to affect the *banian* sales store down my road, at least emotionally! But our funding ask was modest when compared to mass media spends. We were hopeful! Funding positivity, check!

The risks and rewards potentials weren't unlike when we started up in 2003, when more than enough signs said, 'Don't Startup'. This time around, the chances looked better and we could probably succeed. 2010 could win the war for us.

## Hubris

The danger with success is that it can create a feeling of mild invincibility around you. You walk lighter and don't feel so vulnerable easily. Vulnerability makes you defensive, while invincibility makes you drop your defenses.

During a successful period, when the mood and mojo are both high and one faces a seeming difficulty, the way we assess that difficulty is very different from the way we would have earlier, when things weren't so good.

We tend to throw caution to the wind, or at least into a light breeze. Our estimates of our strengths and factors going for us tend to be over. And we always see drawbacks and pitfalls as things that can be easily mitigated by our strengths, instead of analyzing the drawbacks and pitfalls on their own merit.

We fall prey to thinking of ourselves as the king of good times without realizing that good times are but all in the timing. Even kings can fall when the time passes. And time definitely passes by!

Adolf Hitler was a master entrepreneur. He founded a new ideology, marketed it impeccably, was persistent in finding ways to penetrate the market, created a distribution model that was pull driven rather than push, found the right time to enter the market bullishly, converted the ideology into a nation, and then he went international and made (almost) the world his marketplace.

But when you analyze the period of the World War II during 1942–43, you will realize the nature of this entrepreneur's hubris. Hubris is when you are insulated and fortified by success to the extent of feeling undefeatable.

The master strategist and military genius fell prey to rookie mistakes. He took on Russia, who was a silent ally until then; allowed Japan to poke USA, who was a sleeping giant until then; fought on east and west fronts simultaneously, something he himself knew to be the reason for the failure of World War I for Germany; and treated every battle as a final drive to the complete victory of War.

At this point of time he could not take no for an answer from any of his generals because he had been right until then. Success and luck were on his side.

## How is failure looked at in this stage?

Failure is but a mere possibility, not a real tangible threat.

When we are vulnerable we see failure looming over us, and therefore we plan for it. We have a Plan A, a Plan B and even a Plan C. We respect the threat that failure poses and make sure we have our defenses up, along with our courage.

Success removes this feeling of vulnerability from us and our Plan A is our best plan. Plan Bs and Cs don't get designed in such diligent detail and sometimes don't even get designed. Plan B will sometimes be Plan A done more vigorously. When Hitler's Plan A was failing, he merely sent in twice the number of troops to the same place.

Failure is not seen as a symptom for course correction. Failure becomes a bruise to the ego, and therefore letting go or course correction becomes a non-option, because that seems like a sign of weakness.

We hold onto our positions and become stoic and immovable in our approaches. How could we fail? How is that even possible? The world must be wrong, since we are surely right! People who disagree with you become your foes! It becomes impossible to disagree with you. A circle of silence and consonance is built around you, by you. You are well on the path of no return. 1944–45 was the loss of an entrepreneurship that was actually on the threshold of world domination until a few years before.

The 2010 national rollout project was underway. The initial product response was satisfactory after a few initial hiccups and as far as product performance was concerned, it was well on its way to be received well.

The familiar market's response was great and box offices were ringing. But unfamiliar new markets were being remote controlled and it seemed like the battery for the remote wasn't working so well. And what did we do when this happened? Replaced the batteries? Nope. We beat the remote repeatedly in hope that the chemical constituents of the battery would readjust themselves and physically reorient to start re-powering the remote! We beat the remote plenty.

The initial reports from new markets were unhealthy and we beat the remote further. Beating the remote meant that we were in denial that we were failing. How could we fail? We almost felt mildly entitled to succeed! We didn't change our strategy, we merely kept at it. Unfortunately, when our hope funding fell through, our hopes didn't die.

We should have ideally stopped the project right there and cut back on losses. We didn't want to be seen as failing or admit, even to ourselves, that we had failed.

We kept the project powered on its own money and even pumped in more funds when the project was bleeding in parts – refer to Hitler sending twice the number of troops into battles that were being lost. And just like how Hitler never saw those troops again, we never saw those funds again. The project got over as per schedule. Evam was still one of the Top 30 hottest startups, still a YPAE and MTV Youth Icon – all that was true. What was also true was that by end 2010 we were facing our first bankruptcy. We had failed miserably, thanks to our over-dependence on our success.

# Takeouts

**Anti-hubris EQ readiness...**

- When you're successful or are feeling successful, make sure you think of it as a phase.

- Past tactics that got you here are not secret formulae because if you think of them as secret formulae you will never get rid of them when they need to be let gone of. Their sacred nature will make sure you keep repeating them.

- Failures within any project must be treated with respect and processed with due diligence. Every failure is a symptom of something that needs attention.

- Interpret results with objectivity. Keep together a team of Aye and Nay Sayers. Let them feel comfortable expressing themselves. Encourage dissonance. Debate it. And then demand consonance.

- Do mid-campaign course checks and always be open to course corrections. Shed your ego and let the market mould you like water eventually moulds even rock.

- Don't ever feel entitled to success. I will always warn you more about success, than I would of failure because it can actually cause you greater harm.

## Chapter 14

# The Investor

"In the investment seeking process, make sure you
are sold to, as much as you intend to sell."

By 2010–11 our star product was surely bleeding and our
other new products were in a slow growth phase. Most of
our energies had been drained by our over impetus and
over-dependence on our star product and we had been let
down by ourselves mostly. The other products, which had
been carved out by the market (unlike the star product,
which we had carved out of the market), were chugging
along quietly and were showing good response from the
market.

One of these was the behavioral training product
using theatre-based methodologies. Theatre is essentially
a people craft, which means it feeds off the emotional
dynamic of people, and more importantly it thrives on

the emotional dynamic between people, because it is an ensemble craft. Theatre is seldom performed alone, even the smallest productions have a large number of people coming together to create a communion. It is these interpersonal dynamics that have to be managed to create a resonance within and thereby seek a resonance with an eventual audience.

Theatre based methodologies could be used in any workforce to bring about a certain cohesion in working towards a goal. Our division called Happy Factory was churning out innovative products that corporates had started using in handling their people culture challenges.

In 2010, a series of workshops was being peculiarly bought by one organization. I say peculiarly because the number of interventions purchased was high for the size of the organization and the level of briefing and testing we were being put through was rather intense and exacting.

We delivered the product to a very high level of satisfaction and then received a lot of feedback from the client. Feedback that made us think further about the scope of the training we provided. We were excited by these inputs, but were wondering about the extent of the involvement from the client. But the interaction was very positive and exciting. We didn't realize it then, but we were being scoped for investments. These clients won our trust and eventually became the first external investors into the Evam journey.

## It takes two to tango...

Usual investment seeking scenarios are the ones where the ideas people eagerly pitch to venture capitalists/funds in the hope to be bought, or invested in. So Return on Investment plans are drawn up, terms of equity participation are laid out, notional valuations are placed in order to be debated and hope and optimism are sold aggressively. It's all about selling yourself to the investor.

First-time entrepreneurs place a lot of value on investments, their quantum and period over which they may be required, etc. But we seldom place that value on the person/orgranization those investments come from-the investor. *Because right or wrong money depends on who the investor is.* And there is no good or bad investor; there are only right or wrong investors, *for you*!

An investor taking equity can only be equated to a marriage, or surely the addition of a critical family member, especially when they get a seat on the board. And therefore, apply all the criteria involved in that arrangement. Both families have to scope each other, compare cultures and social outlooks.

The actual couple has to get to know each other enough to feel comfortable and familiar, to be able to feel like they can commit a lifetime to each other. This would mean asking each other questions based on each one's wants and desires, and confronting all possible fears and reservations. Futures and outlooks have to be discussed, even if the horoscopes don't match, there must be an alignment in vision, or at least a feeling of being in sync. Both parties should appear reasonable to each other. All this means is that in the investment seeking process *make sure you are sold to,* as much as you intend to sell.

Sell yourself well, proudly. But a greater exhibition of pride and security is when you demand, *respectfully,* that the investor sell to you why they believe that they are the right investor for your startup, why they are the right money and the right partner to have along on your journey. Insist on this respectfully, and your pride will be interpreted as self-respect. If it is done with entitlement, it will be interpreted as arrogance. This will help build a *dialogue* between the potential partners and you, and it will begin the journey of several *reasonable conversations* that will determine the journey of the brand in the future.

Believe me there are tough times ahead and you are going to want to have the investors see your perspective and also feel secure enough to share with you some uncomfortable truths and pieces of advice. They have parked their wealth with you, and that's, by no means, anything less than valuable. And you are allowing them to share one of the greatest dreams of your life – that is invaluable.

I remember sitting in the meetings with the investor and not even grasping that they were willing to invest in us. Call it middle-class modesty, stupidity or just plain ignorance. I remember Sunil nudging me from my stupor of ignorance during the meetings and reminding me to stop asking 'Why' and 'What for' too often. He even feared that I will convince them not to invest in us. That was the density of my unawareness. But what it seemed like to the investor was that there was a good cop and a bad cop and honestly as clever as that tactic sounds, it was completely unintended. It was more like neutral cop and dumb cop. But we had the unique opportunity of being solicited by investors when we didn't even have a need for it. The need was created in our discussions with the investors. The investors were in fact keen to explore the idea and help us see where all it could go. We truly felt energized by their confidence in the idea, and in us, and in their strategic inputs into the realization of them.

This product called 'Happy Factory' became a training boutique enterprise called Evam's Training Sideways - a sideways look at training! It was born in 2012 and by 2014 it was going to save us from a deep abyss. I would wish you investors like our first investors but I do believe that it was a marriage made in heaven!

# Takeouts

- Don't just see the pitch to an investor as a sale that needs to be made. Make sure that you are sold to as well. This is a value match process.

- There is no right or wrong money, it all depends on who the investor is. There is only a right or wrong investor, for you.

- An investor is to be treated as an entrant to your family. So make sure due diligence is done and all the trust is built before the red carpet is laid out.

# Quality: Listening

There is something called the Circle of Silence in communication theory – where a leader builds a coterie of people who generally agree with them, around themselves. More aye sayers than naysayers and after a point the naysayers will vanish, because saying nay will be taken as dissonance, betrayal and then they will unsubscribe. Leaving behind a circle of silence, a silent group of people who define themselves as being in agreement with the leader. They may disagree on small details, but that would be more to show that they are involved but they never ever disagree on strategic points.

All entrepreneurs face resistance from the world – the market, their family, the ecosystem, banks, customers even. And therefore they tend to build, within their own Batcaves, a safe haven for ideating in peace. And therefore within the four walls of the Batcave it becomes difficult to allow any violent resistance. The entrepreneur will tend to hire people who resemble themselves. This is one form of narcissism or insecurity. By hiring associates like ourselves we negate the opportunity of diversity in opinion and create an artificial sense of calm and consonance. We tend to treat something different from ourselves as alien!

As more success comes your way you will become more insulated from voices that disagree with you. And with great failure people will feel bad to disagree with you. Hire and keep people who are very different from each other and surely from you in your team. Actively encourage the naysayers because each time a Nay is sounded, it is certainly not easy. I am saying don't make it easy. Make it easier or at least less difficult. Do not express your opinion on anything up top – be the last to express an opinion – or better still leave them guessing about what you actually feel about something. Let them mull over what you may be thinking. Don't show any bias towards one opinion. Play the devil's advocate and then jump again as the angel's counsel. Let every side be heard and debated.

The bigger the organization and older the startup, the farther away it is from the customer and the market. You don't know the market anymore, you only know your involvement in the market. In such cases market truths will come only in the form of results. To wait for results and find out the truth is a rather expensive exercise. Therefore it's better to debate everything within the four walls of the Batcave and to debate everything you need to listen to everything.

And beware of the greatest liar- yourself! Question every single thing you believe in and may the answers strengthen your belief. If left unquestioned, it's weak and only gets weaker! Allow the first bullet of doubt upon yourself. Set an example!

Chapter 15

# Success & Failure

*"Fear of failure is a greater fear than failure itself."*

2008, 5 years into the Evam journey, was the year we were nominated for MTV Youth Icons. It was a nomination, followed by public vote for the finalists selections and we made the list. I suspect we were the funnest entity to vote for, because nothing else could explain the huge number of votes we got. Because the last few years saw winners like 'Orkut' (yes, the entire company) and MSD (I will not expand these iconic initials).

2008 was the year we were declared one of the Top 30 Hottest Startups from businesses across India by the TATA NEN foundation. We were the only arts-based startup, while everyone else was either in IT or Retail, or the newly emerging social entrepreneurship space. I remember sitting in a hall filled with eager entrepreneurs, business pundits and venture funds and wondering what we were doing there! I remember someone asking me what was our EBITDA (Earnings before Interest, Tax, Depreciation and Amortisation) and I remember telling him that we had never done any musicals on stage, convinced he meant Evita!

But 2008 was also the year we had branched out into exploring new business lines such as training corporates using arts-based methodologies, teaching wannabe actors acting, etc. This was desperation, according to many pundits, because it was taking us away from the core of what performing arts is seen to be - performance! Were we desperate to survive and be glorious on our own mettle? Yes. Were we desperate to make money however we could? Not really. We needed it to be sustainable and had to create methodologies that were true to us. But were we failing without it? Yes.

2009 saw us becoming India winners for YPAE (Young Performing Arts Entrepreneurs) and representing India at the World finals held at Edinburgh. These were the first VISA stamps on our passport. But 2009 also saw us embarking on our last ditch attempt at saving our Box Office Revenue based business model. We put all our strengths and resources into it like one last surge. We were surely in trouble then. 2013 saw us being announced for eight nominations for METAs, a very prestigious national theatre critics award and winning in two categories. 2013 also saw us nursing the commercial wounds of having produced the national award-winning production, which took us towards our second bankruptcy.

I remember receiving, on the morning of each of these awards, several congratulatory messages and glorious press coverage. And it always took me a second to wonder what they were congratulating us about because with every moment of success there has always the looming presence of a failure that we were handling, trying to keep house in order.

## Treat the two imposters just the same

"If you can meet with Triumph and Disaster, and treat the two imposters just the same."

These are words from an immortal poem *If* by Rudyard Kipling. It says that success and failure are probably two sides of the same coin – opposite in effect maybe, but of the same essence. They are to be treated with equanimity, because both are probably mirages.

I have known this about success. There is that moment of success that is apparent to the world, post which you are flooded with congratulatory messages and well wishes. This adds a buzz and a glow to the brand in the market, for a little while. This glow is much like the fluorescent materials that gain incandescence when placed closed to a light, an afterglow of a bright spark. But they have to be periodically recharged to keep them glowing. Success is a constant pursuit. You keep craving for more.

True success is actually very personal – when something that you thought to be difficult to achieve, but were working on nonetheless, suddenly finds the hope of realization and results start trickling in. This is the most rewarding moment of success. A meeting that went well where the other partner saw the solution just the way you wanted them to. A proposal that falls through, but leads to a bigger opportunity elsewhere. These moments are mostly personal and they're difficult for the world, beyond the core group, to understand.

The pursuit of success is a journey of optimism and confidence. It is fraught with risk and the promise of rewards. Entrepreneurs are not gamblers. They take calculated risks. They acknowledge the risk, the roadblocks and believe, rightly or not, in the plans they have to mitigate it and the strength of their own character to mitigate them, and all the while believing positively that it will pull through. This optimism is intrinsic.

Success is not an end. It is several little pit stops. Celebrating it like it's the end will be as absurd a race car driver getting out of the car, to celebrate at a pit stop. The pursuit of success postures us to the best possible finesse, preparedness and shape. Whether success is achieved or not, you would have anyway gotten to be a better version of yourself along with the organization.

I have known this about failure. It is more frequent than success. If success and failure were cyclical, then they would occur in equal measure. That is not so. Failure is more frequent than success.

Failure is indicative of an attempt, and therefore analysis of the failure has to measure the attempt and fine tune it, rather than the result. If the attempt was as per plan, then that should be celebrated with the team; while the core group has to acknowledge failure of strategy and rethink. The attempt is everything and every team is responsible for only making the attempt error-free and genius-filled. The result is for the core team to ponder over.

Fear of failure is a greater fear than failure itself. Fear of failure inhibits confidence and makes one overly defensive.

It is like walking and working inside a dark room, always fearing the unknown. Because if you accept the darkness, you will at least invent the light bulb. Where confidence and optimism are in short measure, it is possible that the attempt will be weak and defensive, and failure could be self-prophesying.

Make failure a friend. Become familiar with it – in the sense that, know how to look it in the eye and find out more about it. All our lives we are taught to run away from it, or dispel it, or simply be in denial. Denial is like the ostrich burying its head in the sand – we can all see its naked backside.

Failure is how you interpret it – hence it's very subjective. The world will declare the nature of what they believe the failure is. But it is possible that it may be something altogether different. Because they have seen only the result, while you are aware of the process. The best chance for a truthful analysis lies with you. Equip yourself with the world's perspective, as well as your truth, and analyze what went wrong. It's not this or that – it's about being objective.

Failure can be fun if you think of it as the best way to get the truth out of the market, or your own organization. If you are willing to listen and process failure, it can be the best friend. Failure is not the end. It has several significant pit stops. Grieve it, but process it - don't sweep it away. Allow it to be remembered, once processed.

Over the years, Evam has had several operational failures within several projects- Late deliveries, inefficient solutions, disappointed clients. These came from unreasonable deadlines, human error, trust failures, bad luck, poor planning, unfavourable market conditions, etc. These kinds of failures will repeat themselves and you will learn to deal with them better. Dealing with them is addressing them, and assuring the customer/ client, and working harder to make the solution work. Things do go wrong, it's all about how one deals with it.

How the organization deals with it is 'character.' Most clients have forgiven an error, but have never forgotten how we reacted. How we reacted has been remembered and recounted, favourably or not, depending on how mature and responsible the reactions and resolutions were. Bigger failures are those that lead to loss of spirit or confidence. The two bankruptcies weren't easy on the middle-class spirit of Evam's founders. The first one was because we had not figured out a sustainable business model yet so were had thrown everything at it to find one. We survived this one by discovering humility. We accepted our faults and were humbled by the results. We became quieter and calmer entrepreneurs. Brash bullishness was replaced by quiet confidence backed by preparation.

The second one was heavy. I remember the core team regrouping and asking the really tough questions- Is this the end of the road? Should we officially give up? Will we regret walking away from this, at this point of time? What do we have left to work on? Is it enough? Is it sustainable? Do we have it in us?

We built the businesses back from scratch. We took the losses upon ourselves. And worked intelligently rather than too hard, which means we worked hard on the 'right' products and kept all other 'less right' products and projects in the back burner. We worked without ego, and never let anyone else's perceptions about us hurt us because it wasn't time to listen to the world, it was time to listen to ourselves and put our heads down and climb back up to cash positives and reserves. We had a close family member take over the reins of managing finances and believe me if there is one piece of financial advice I would give you, it is 'ask dad how to do it.' Not all dads have money but all dads know what the threats of zero balance are and saving up for a rainy day is like. I am not being sexist here when I say dad because I know a lot of moms who are dads in this regard.

Nothing makes money in the long term like disciplined financial practices. I have always known how to create value. But keeping it and allowing it to multiply on its own is another science by itself. Products don't always make money. Money makes the most money. If you ever have money lying around please put it to work. Not all reserves have to become new projects. Don't be trigger happy on new projects during modest times. The second bankruptcy renewed our spirits. We were back to zero and born again in our year 11. Evam was 1.1 again.

# Takeouts

- True success is actually very personal.

- The pursuit of success is a journey of optimism and confidence.

- Success is not an end. It is several little pit stops.

- The pursuit of success postures us to the best possible finesse, preparedness and shape.

- Failure is more frequent than success.

- Failure is indicative of an attempt, and therefore analysis of the failure has to measure the attempt and fine tune it, rather than the result.

- Fear of failure is a greater failure than failure itself.

- Failure is how you interpret it, hence it's very subjective.

Chapter 16

# Innovation

"And in entrepreneurship staying down is never an
option. You have to dust it off and move on."

One thing about failure is that it's humbling. It makes you
look at yourself more realistically.

Falling down could be circumstantial, but staying
down is a choice. And in entrepreneurship staying down is
never an option. You have to dust it off and move on.

Our national rollout failure in 2010 saw us forced into
a corner. And usually creativity comes from being pushed
into corners. This is the innovation I have known. Whenever
I see giant organizations have a separate innovation cell it
makes me wonder two things- one is that they recognize
innovation as a critical part of their process and secondly,
they see innovation as apart from basic operations.

At Evam, innovation has always come from necessity. I remember during the recession of 2008–09 when live entertainment was low in the consumer pecking order of priorities we had a situation of lots of seats going vacant. We didn't bring down the price because we had worked very hard to create that value proposition, but instead launched a scheme called SaM – Seats are Money. Every unsold seat was monetized or utilized – how? We auctioned these unsold seats at discounted special rates to crowdfunding where people donated money for an underprivileged student to watch an English play. We called loyal audiences and made them +1 their purchase for a friend they wanted to gift a seat to – this made our loyal customer happy and introduced someone to theatre. Recession was tided over with smartness.

In 2010 we were in the unique predicament of having to create a play with minimum actors, No costumes or set, no script, which we had to pay licenses for, no tech requirements such as lights and effects, and no auditorium hire – basically no money, but something had to be done. This is like telling a film crew to make a movie with minimum actors, self-scripts, and no camera! We created a 'play' with one actor, self-scripted autobiographical, chose a genre that was comedy in order to be popular, with only two lights on stage, and the stage was in a buffet restaurant, not in an auditorium. We called it 'Urban Turban, Tall Tales from the Top of our Head!' We had been pushed into a corner and we innovated! We had no idea what we had created for ourselves. Years later they called it 'Standup Comedy.'

## Cornered Tigers...

Entrepreneurship in the startup phase is all about moving the operations into a certain predictability and stability. Business models that are stable are more valuable than peaks and troughs, which are unpredictable. In this search for stability we sometimes forget that the greatest inventions are born from disruptions. And as far as disruptions go, there will be no shortage of it in your startup phase. When things don't go your way, however hard you may have tried, it's time to accept the market reality and adapt. This will create a new version of the product/solution more in tune with market needs. This forced innovation and need to innovate is something you must tune your team to become accepting of. Otherwise each time a result comes in that is different from what was expected, there could be a pall of gloom and disappointment in the team. Results are a journey – there is no end to the cycle of success and failure, like I said in the previous chapter. Each result is the stepping stone for the next input.

Large organizations force themselves into corners and simulate situations of scarcity. Startups operate on scarcity. Use the scarcity to toughen up.

It seemed like a huge step down for theatre/plays to come into dingy pubs, and buffet restaurants and un-auditoriums. Auditoriums have their own aura and charm, technical equipment, spotlights, all the bells and whistles. We used to have to go into a pub/cafe and then find a corner, put up our own platform, focus a few lights and then perform first to win the attention of the audience before we could even seek to entertain them.

I can't tell you how difficult that was for us but truly the logistical challenge of it felt more difficult than the spiritual comedown it was. We were doing literally anything to stay in the game and others saw it as a fall from grace, not only for ourselves, but for theatre/drama at large. I can only tell you this- *all is fair in love, war and entrepreneurship.* Love is needed to start a war and war is needed to win love. Love is Feeling, War is Action.

At Evam we have two qualities that we consider the DNA of the organization- imagination and rigour. Imagination is a feeling and rigour is the effort taken to realize the feeling. If we didn't have rigour we would be perennial dreamers, which the world will eventually stop taking seriously. And if you didn't have imagination then you would never start envisioning possibilities in the first place.

You are your dream, and the effort to realize it.

We kept at it. We called it Solo Comedy Theatre. One year later Standup Comedy was something India began to discover for itself and we were already 2 years ahead of the curve. 'Evam Standup Tamasha' was born as a brand and Evam became the best incubators of stand-up talent on this side of the Vindhyas. We were creators, producers, managers and entrepreneurs in this space. We didn't expect this movement to blow up to this size but we were willing to back it because of the corner that the market has forced us into. This felt like a courageous fight back, while acknowledging the prowess of the market, but never backing down into inaction.

This, along with Training Sideways, were the brands that sailed us out of startup mode and into Act III.

# Takeouts

- Greatest inventions are born from disruptions, and scarcity is the greatest disruption. Make it your friend.

- Accepting market realities will make you adapt and version your product.

- Forced innovation and need to innovate is something you must tune your team to become accepting of.

- You are your dream, and the effort to realize it.

# Act III

## Chapter 17

# Grown up

"The talents required to navigate calm seas are very different from those that are useful to manage choppy, rough ones."

2014–18 Evam had a uniquely different set of challenges. We had pulled ourselves into the 'grown-up' phase of being a startup, and could no longer actually call ourselves a 'startup.' But having moved from choppy waters to deep, but calmer seas felt very different indeed.

We had divisions growing organically - Happy Cow, our children's educational division, started off while we were neck deep in operational issues during the 'adolescent' phase; Evam Standup Tamasha, our comedy brand, which had started in the late infant-early adolescent phase on the heels of our first bankruptcy; Sideways Training, our arts methodology based behavioral training division, which got invested into right in the middle of our difficult times, prior to our second breaking point.

Growing each division, which we realize will soon become full-fledged businesses of their own, took a different mettle altogether. We had just moved from a phase where we were hungry and foraging for food, into suddenly becoming well and regularly fed, and even becoming providers of food! This was all too sudden, just like all growing up is about.

2014–18 has seen us become Evam 1.1, which was very different from being a startup! In this Act III, I will tell you about this phase very briefly. Briefly because this book is largely about starting up, and also because I don't believe starting up is a one-time phase in the life of an entrepreneurship. I will also tell you about qualities that you should look out for, which will hold you in good stead through your startup journey, and as reminders to myself as well, of that phase.

The talents required to navigate calm seas are very different from those that are useful to manage choppy, rough ones. War time tactics come more naturally to some cultures that have seen long strife of war and for them peace time is seen as an eventual happy ending, and when it does finally arrive, it leaves them wondering how they can handle it.

All our tactics of the startup phase became almost redundant during this 'Grown up' phase, and everything changed: We could no longer be excessively disruptive, we had to become patient instead and investing into systems and ongoing product research. We had to huddle together less frequently to discuss tactics. We just had to meet twice a year *to reflect on strategy.* We no longer had to lose sleep over winning clients; we had to redirect that effort to *keeping clients,* and even letting go of 'wrong' ones.

Dependence on product selling shifted to brand marketing, because word-of-mouth and brand awareness was the better way to keep building a business in this phase. Feedback from clients that had earlier led to frequent changes of product, now changed to dealing with the *clients' needs and understanding those better.* Cash reserves existed now! We had to figure what to use those for! We had more access to funding, debt or equity, as we chose it. We had to *invest in our existing talent and human resources to become better*, rather than just quicker. They had to genuinely become better at what they did! We could suddenly hire well-trained talent, instead of just hiring raw resources and having to train them extensively. We had to start thinking of everything a year in advance, rather than go quarter to quarter or sometimes, as we used to, even month to month. We had to seriously focus on our vision now and see how we needed to align ourselves to it. This Vision/Mission was the toughest chapter at business school because one could hardly spot the difference between them or understand what they each were.

Asking a young person what they want to be when they grow up is rarely a valuable exercise, except for maybe, amusing oneself. I remember truly wanting to be a traffic constable. I now felt like I had to give a more serious and better answer without exactly knowing what it was. What was Evam's Vision beyond 'survival?' We have been running on this mode for the last 4 years now (as of 2018), and I must confess that calm seas are extremely comforting. Taking our hands off the wheel and auto pilot-ing are extravagances we have been able to afford as founders and CEOs in this phase.

They say that bringing up children is difficult, but one does so, hoping that one day that they will take care of the parents. Whether this is true about parenting or not, this has happened to me with my entrepreneurship. In phases of difficulty, in my personal life even, Evam has been a source of solace and strength and a reminder of the value that has been created. That baby that I created had begun supporting me! The responsibility I feel now is of a different nature. I suddenly feel even more responsible and here's why.

During difficult times even the most ridiculously poor moves can be written off as owing to the nature of the times and will get buried under the avalanche of chaos that defines this period. I am sure I have made many errors during those difficult times that were completely overlooked.

But during calm times even a mild wrong gear shift can cause everyone to notice and wonder, if the captain has his bearings in place. You can imagine how it would be to do anything that causes the ship grave danger in this period. Every move of mine is going to have repercussions for these divisions, and either going to aid or impede their full development into businesses. Decisions points are fewer but I need much more than just instinct to answer them right. I feel more responsible and this is new! Let me share with you some dilemmas we face as founders and where we stand with respect to those.

# Takeouts

- Moving out of startup phase into a more predictable steady state of business poses its own unique challenges.

- It's time to start looking into the future and be able to predict the next turning points, rather than just focusing on the battles of the moment.

- Visioning and strategy become more important than quarterly targets and tactics.

- Every decision, from brand positioning, winning new business, keeping an existing client, hiring a new recruit etc, has to be looked at from a sustainability perspective and how it is going to make the brand and the business look in the face of tomorrow.

- Today's peace should go beyond the chaos of survival of yesterday, into the glory that lies in the tomorrow.

Chapter 18

# Dilemmas

"All miracles are relative; relative to the world
in which you operate."

This short chapter covers some key dilemmas that an
entrepreneur will face during the course.

## To scale or not to scale?

Evam has not figured scale yet, and 15 years in now, we
have only just started to seriously think about it. The first
thing about scale that seemed exciting to us as younger
Entrepreneurs, was the sheer bigness of being big. Big
seemed to impress people, and throwing topline figures in
the higher crores, seemed like an easy way to park ourselves
into anyone's mind space. Big would buy us attention and
influence.

But the key thing one should realize about big is that big is relative. What you would kill yourself creating to make big, could be 'small to medium' only depending on who you are in the company of. I have been to many entrepreneurship forums where people were interested more in how, in spite of our modest topline figures, we were grabbing so much attention. This was because of the nature of the industry we were working in, and all miracles are relative; relative to the world in which you operate.

To scale or not to scale should only depend on how the road looks ahead, and how smooth the drive is and if it is thumbs up on both counts then feel free to accelerate. But if the terrain is uncertain and or if the vehicle is suspect, then acceleration is but a shot in the dark. To attempt to scale when the house or market is not in order, is committing *hara-kiri.*

If the business model has reached steady state with a modest predictable growth, and this is usually exhibited by a sense of calm in operations, and divisions working in sync with each other, then by all means shake the boat and scale up. Your ship can take the surge forward.

If the market is beckoning growth and scale is achievable, then this is less reason to scale, although it seems like a good enough reason to. The reason to scale then is to make hay while the sun shines. But if the operations and internal housekeeping have been chaotic, this impetus could only add more chaos to the system. More money amidst chaos usually will lead to mishandling of money, and improper appreciation and accounting for value created.

## To be rich or to be king?

Entrepreneurship is seeking ownership of your own time and energy, and hoping to do so with your wealth as well. The only piece of 'life' real estate you will own in your life will be your entrepreneurship. It will be your safe space, and it's your job to also make it a challenging space for you. But it is the real estate where your word is most valued, and therefore the worth of your word is what you are fully responsible for. It is a heady feeling to be the king of an ecosystem, hopefully not in a power trip kind of way, but more in a protective responsible way.

In the race to be rich, this authority will be severely threatened, and your need to hold onto this piece of real estate will be tested. Riches can't be achieved without incorporating more partners into the ecosystem – investors, associates, client partners, board of directors and maybe even a new CEO.

All this will make your authority much lesser, and surely that should be the desired outcome – holding onto control will limit the riches that can be accrued and this will make anyone from the outside less open to work with your organization. If the decision-making system in your organization is done post debating, consensus-seeking and then executed with certainty, then you will be more prone to having partners lock onto you. Whereas if the process was autocratic, singular and whimsical, then however wise you may actually be, the partners would perceive it as unsafe. You will still remain king, but not get richer as you possibly could.

Evam has enjoyed being the king for the longest time, and we believe that it's time to tread the path of riches ahead. But the awareness that it's one or the other or surely one more than the other always is critical.

Chapter 19

# Right & Left-brained

"What makes an entrepreneur special is the bridge
of intelligence between the left and the right
brain, the bridge between Business and Art."

I am writing this chapter having just gotten off a
rigorous yearly meeting with Evam's auditor and it left
me wondering. Being compliant to all the mandatory
accounting and accountability practices is a lot of systemic
work. It's making sure the system reports back on tangible
real numbers, and then documenting them, filing them,
collating them, uploading them and then using that tool to
measure, analyze and keep track. It astounds me that, while
running a business, it is not just your job to do great work
in a way where it gets valued and paid for, it's also equally
important to file it, document it, report back, be compliant
and then after all is done and pennies are counted, you pay

yourself the value for your labour. It seems like a lot of hard work, doesn't it?

There will be things that need to be done rigorously and repeatedly in an entrepreneurship. This can become tiring, laborious and tedious. At Evam we have had the unique advantage of being in the business of the arts, which means it is a business for sure, but the core product is the arts.

Business and science appeal to and utilize one part of your being that is rational, methodical, incremental and repeatable. This is a very valuable skill, to be good at these things and ensure systems rigorously execute these kinds of activities. But too much of this can lead to fatigue and breakdown.

The arts is more sensorial, fun, random and thrives on imagination and even unpredictability. Whenever we do too many rigorous tasks, we get to experience the magic and emotional power of the arts, because it is our core product. This shifts the mood of the organization since it utilizes a different part of your being.

At Evam we try and understand the human perspective of every issue, the emotional angle and its imaginative exposition. This is the arts. This we do through stories, playshops (as opposed to workshops), comedy, simulations and games etc. Therefore we get to do all the usual rigorous activities in an organization like finance, systems, payroll, accounts, vendor registrations, audits and filing taxes. But at the same time we get to ideate, create, make art, make mistakes, laugh, think, feel and also measure ourselves on the emotional impact of our artistic products.

At Evam we take this for granted, because its core to our way of operating. We have an equal activation of our left and right brain parts of our being! What makes an entrepreneur special is the bridge of intelligence between the left and the right brain, the bridge between Business and Art.

Is great entrepreneurship an Art or Science? It is in fact both.

A straight line may not be the only way to connect two dots, it can also mean adding another plane and seeing the dots merge into one. I think I just got metaphysical in my imagery. But even metaphysics is basically that, physics with imagination.

Most great ideas of solving a problem will come from the entrepreneurs who have experienced the problem, and then exposed themselves to different experiences, different from those at work, and suddenly answers will find their way. Staying in the same circumstances of the problem rarely helps you find an innovative solution. It requires distancing yourself and changing the mood of the mind. I get the best business ideas and solutions for problems at work, when I'm traveling on leisure. I have stood before the Colosseum and said, 'Eureka,' because I got an idea for solving our cash flow issues in a particularly difficult project. I wasn't thinking hard about the issue, but I had definitely internalized it enough for an answer to emerge when the mood and surrounding was different.

A lot of young startups are going to have a lot of work and rational challenges ahead of them. I would mostly advise anyone starting up *to* take up an art form or sport, and also share something artistic with the team. This will lead to a different energy being brought into play between the people, and it will surely lead to several breakthroughs at work, and within the team. Great entrepreneurship is always at the cusp of being a Science and an Art and what one can't solve only the other can. Allow both these parts of your being to be alert in this journey at all times. And startup is a phase where emotions run high, and hence the emotional energy of a startup has to be harnessed and channeled effectively. Use it to motivate, to bring together, to bond and to help achieve what one would think of as impossible.

The bigger the organization, the more antiseptic it gets, where emotional energy is feared and very often, even muted in the name of being 'professional.' A startup should use this advantage positively. Great entrepreneurship is therefore both an Art and a Business. Emotional energies of the organization have to be awoken and prudent business strategies have to harness their release.

# Quality: The Big Boss

One of the advantages of having your own startup is that you get to bypass the greatest evil predicament in the professional human being world out there, the bad boss! Bad bosses are responsible for every magnificent opportunity and job to suddenly seem bleak and hopeless, and worth giving up. Bad bosses are mood spoilers and make you believe that you are not worth much, which in turn reflects on your daily life and then things all spiral downwards from there.

The good news about starting up? *You have no Big Bad Boss!* The bad news? *You are probably the Big Bad Boss.* To become a leader of people too soon in life, in terms of age and experience, is never an easy thing. And it's more difficult for people working with you, rather than yourself. Bosses seldom get to hear honest feedback from the people working for them, and especially in a startup, where HR departments and feedback systems are low on priority, feedback for you as a boss is non-existent.

Being a good boss is much like being a parent. Like there is no organized feedback system for how good a parent one is, similarly how good or bad a boss you are, will be a blind spot. Therefore let's see what parents do to become better parents? First-time parents tend to read up a lot on how to be good parents. They glean from good practices of their own parents and see how they want to deploy that themselves. They ensure what they thought were bad practices of their own parents to never creep into their space. They listen to the child and ensure that they figure a unique meaningful reaction each time, and keep this learning process ongoing and constant. They compare notes with other parents and gauge how they handle things.

All this is do-able by you to become a better boss to your people, without taking the analogy literally, your employees are not your children, although you are responsible for them. Like children to parents, they are at your mercy, and are subject to your best judgment of things. Be the best boss you can be.

## Here are some things to keep in mind:

- Be a friend to everyone, but don't be too friendly. A boss being a friend cannot mean that the rapport becomes too personal. *It is always a professional engagement first and foremost.*

- *Listen more than you talk.* Talk when the forum is one to many. Listen when the forum is one on one.

- Listen when the forum is people talking in groups - be the silent listener there.

- Don't have the same approach to everyone. Deal with different personalities differently and there will be some kinds of people who you understand better than others. Make an effort, therefore, to work better with people who you don't understand easily.

- *Deal with everyone fairly* – fairness is the same for all! Don't play favorites.

- Think of being a boss as a skill that you need to keep getting better at, like entrepreneurship itself.

- Share your people challenges with peers who are bosses themselves and surely even more with people who have been bosses for much longer than you. Their wisdom will be invaluable.

- Realize that Human Resources are not easy to replace. And a good human resource is probably impossible to replace.

- People don't quit jobs – *they quit their bosses.*

- Don't always desire to be liked by your employees but please don't ever be disliked. If you have bad news, makes sure you say it, sensitively. Don't keep quiet. Or don't make bad news seem like what it's not, good news!

- Talk to your people often and motivate the spirit of the organization.

- They are looking to you for that, whether you like it or not.

Chapter 20

# The Inner Entrepreneur

"Entrepreneurs have to rent the red carpets and roll them out themselves, for themselves."

Before we conclude the book, let me confront the uncomfortable uncertainty that may lie before you – is there an entrepreneur in you? Do you have it in you to journey into the unknown before you?

Let's answer this. How employable are you? How ideal are you as a hire and are you likely to be hired? And how would you feel being hired as a professional in a steady job?

What about an entrepreneur makes them an ideal hire?

- They are self-driven.

- They find a way to solve a problem, with minimum guidance.

- They don't need to be monitored constantly.

- They act like bosses so they marshal all available resources.

- They don't fear asking for more, or just asking.

- They take up a task as a challenge that needs to be overcome.

- They are more driven by the work, rather than the remuneration.

- They don't like it too easy. They like being challenged.

- They go beyond their work profiles and beyond their call of duty.

- They are excited by the trust imposed on them and act responsibly.

What about an entrepreneur makes for them to be *un-ideal to be hired?*

- They hate being monitored constantly. They need their space and leeway.

- They hate too many instructions. They may hate existing procedures and find them redundant.

- They hate being questioned too often.

- They won't stay within their work profiles and will act like bosses!

- They will ask for more.

- They constantly need challenges and will wither in the absence of that constant stimulation.

- They hate not being trusted.

I have probably stated similar reasons for why an entrepreneurial personality is ideal/un-ideal to be hired by a corporation.

But there are two key differences between the two: Financial risk/responsibility appetite and the ability and need to be Self-driven.

An entrepreneur must remain an entrepreneur, if their need to take a financial risk is what drives them and therefore enjoy the responsibility of being master of their own financial destiny. As I said earlier, entrepreneurs aren't gamblers, but they do take calculated risks.

An entrepreneur must remain an entrepreneur, if their ability to be self-driven is actually a need. Which means they hate anyone else driving them. They hate being told what to do, like follow instructions. They will make awful employees!

Try telling Bruce Wayne what he needs to do, and you have lost the do-gooder for good. Try and become a 'sanctioner' of his budgets and restrict his funding, and you will incur the wrath of his dark side. He has to do what he does, by himself, in his own way, and wants to feel fully responsible. No one can reward or even punish him, only he can, himself. Hence, Batman! Whereas, an entrepreneurial person becomes the best kind of person to hire, if they exhibit all such qualities of an entrepreneur but do not prefer the risk appetite of finance. They want to be paid well and valued, and do not enjoy the uncertainty in reward, at the end of doing great work.

And also for those who self-starting is an ability, and definitely not a need. They don't mind instructions and actually work well when they combine their approach with the received instructions, and then mix and match. They don't mind following a set procedure and given timeline, as long as they are trusted to deliver the results. This kind of person is an ideal intrapreneur and that is the most valued kind of individual in the professional world out there. There is no value anymore, for a young person embarking into the professional world, who is only interested in working in a fun company with a cool culture that makes them appear cool as well! A professional identity is no longer just a social accessory.

Recruiters are looking for young people who will define themselves with the work they do, rather than the place they do it at, and are willing to pay them well, provided they deliver. Intrapreneurs deliver results and enjoy being rewarded bonuses and raises based on their performance.

Professional organizations are looking for leaders who can run divisions and micro companies as if they were a business. Maybe you are better suited to be an intrapreneur, in which case there are already red carpets rolled out for you, out there. Entrepreneurs have to rent the red carpets and roll them out themselves, for themselves. If at the end of this chapter, I have made the identity of the intrapreneur seem very exciting, and one that you feel 'sounds too good to be true' and 'ideal,' then maybe there is more of an intrapreneur in you. That may not mean that there is no entrepreneur in you at all – there may be, deep inside. It may need experience, age and time, to pull out and realize itself. But nothing can readily prepare you for a financial risk and result/reward appetite. That is the unknown that one needs to accept in the journey. There are no guarantees in Life, Love and Entrepreneurship.

So, maybe, until then, **'Don't Startup.'**

# Random Advice

- Travel.

- Treat close friends and family well during your startup days. Especially those who are understanding of your chaotic schedules. Be grateful for their tolerance. Their tolerance is affording you peace.

- Make sure you pay yourself well and regularly. Not paying yourself is okay for the 'adolescent' startup phase when you may be cash-strapped. But once revenues kick in start the discipline of paying yourself, and keep increasing that payment as the company grows. Don't NOT do this. Don't be modest, or take yourself for granted.

- Don't pay yourself too much. Let that come from profits may be.

- You will get bored lots. So please do find a hobby.

- Find a life partner who allows you your space – because your entrepreneurship will mostly be your space.

- But also realize that it should never come at the expense of them. In your personal life put your family first, and at work put your people first. You have already put yourself first by choosing to be on your own journey. Therefore remember to do this.

# Random Advice

- Travel. Travel. Travel.

- Go out there and meet other people who are starting up and please don't do it as networking. Genuinely try and connect with a few and learn from their journeys as you allow them to learn from yours. Networking is purely selfish and you will already have enough of that within the pursuit of your business.

- The society and the world around you came before you and your entrepreneurship – so you do always owe them big time as does your entrepreneurship.

- Keep fit. After an age your body and your mind will resemble each other.

- Don't fear what you don't know. Always suspect what you think you know for certain. Entertain doubt. Enjoy uncertainty.

- Lead by example. Follow rules, especially those that you have laid out.

- Don't expect it to be easy. Don't lament about how difficult it is.

- Do good. Be fair. But fight like a champion.

# Afterword

I called this book *Don't Startup* because it's provocative. Provocative not to everyone, but to that entrepreneur inside you. Entrepreneurial personalities hate being told not to do something, and how it cannot be done, and how it is not worth doing. They don't walk away from a don't, they engage with it. Engage, because it is a reflection of an inner fear, which is also saying don't. Therefore engaging with a don't is a way to engage with yourself and your inner voice that needs to be communicated with. The greater the resistance the more is the curiosity to seek. And the journey of entrepreneurship itself is an eternal fight against the tide so if the ride is all about resistance, then might as well start with a don't. This is not the first don't you will hear, so get used to it.

As I write this last chapter in the book, I am anxious to leave even after having said all that I need to say and I still fear that I may have left something out. Because as much as these words are meant for you, they are meant for me and Evam as well.

This book was an effort to recollect a phase of Evam's journey that one calls the 'startup' phase, which we have moved away from in the last 5 years.

The last 5 years have been about stability, growth and order. We have had divisions that have become steady and are powering forth into their own destinies in the market. Overheads have become predictable and market results are less surprising and more stable. This has brought much-needed peace and leeway to explore plans that had to remain in the back burner, until now.

But this also means that the organization has become slightly too comfortable and maybe even less risk-taking. The first time you break a bone it teaches you pain and then leaves behind a healed bone, and along with it, fear. This fear of an impending pain inhibits our ability to leap without abandon.

We market more than we sell. We plan more than we do. We ruminate before we sanction, and we sanction only after questioning. We hate surprises. We think we know, and that we ought to. We have grown up and that's saying something.

But the startup phase has its unique advantages that make it distinctly different from where we are now. Startup posturing is very agile, and hungry. There is an athletic need to pounce on every opportunity and most things one does are approached from first principles. Everything is invented, until later this becomes 'this is how we do things here.' Doing everything for the first time makes one familiar with unfamiliarity. Everything is a surprise and surprises aren't to be feared.

I wrote this book to recount that phase, and to remind myself of it, because that phase for Evam is going to be round the corner again. If you are reading this book in its first run (and yes i am assuming that this book will have multiple print runs - optimism is an entrepreneurial bug!), then we will be embarking upon an ambitious launch of a division of ours, into a full-fledged company status and entering it into orbit in its 'startup phase.'

Life doesn't afford you many youths, and once you age its irreversible!

*Entrepreneurship on the other hand gives you many lives* – it's your choice to go back and again be an infant and an adolescent and then grow up all over again. And no two lives will be the same.

Your entrepreneurship itself must see many startup phases, because it renews your energy and your commitment to going back to zero and starting again.

15 years of Evam and it has been quite a ride. I often think of that younger version of me who kickstarted this, and I'm filled with gratitude for the temperament and the ecosystem in which he had this dream. It takes a

comfortable bed, a happy thought, reassurance, the right temperature, and imagination to 'dream' well – and a lifetime of rigour to realize it! Did Evam become the dream we originally had?

Evam started out to selfishly and passionately realize a way of life where the founders got to do what they loved doing, and over the years it has morphed into an enterprise of 42 people who are all working doing the same for themselves. This is no longer the founders' dream – it's everybody else's too. And I hope yours as well.

Because if there is one thing I would wish you, it would be to *do what you love doing* and all that you love doing, as many times as possible, within this lifetime. And to do so lifelong in these modern times, one will have to make a living out of that thing you love doing. You, your family, your society all should be able to relate to it and get from it, in order for this attachment to last a lifetime.

But as you struggle with your startup or the dream of it, just remember that you are part of an elite blessed lot that has ventured into a path hitherto unknown, to discover it all by yourself. And along with you, many are doing the same, and I wish each and every one of you a journey as memorable as Evam's, as I wish myself and Evam just the same, with our new journey right now.

So because life is short and you live only once, pretend there was no choice, and **Go Startup!**

*You are your dream. So dream well and realize it responsibly. Imagination and Rigour!*

# About the Author

Karthik Kumar has many first generation startups, in all his avatars – entrepreneur, standup comic, film actor, speaker and now writer. But his most prized 'startup' avatar is being the co-founder of Evam, an arts-based entrepreneurship. You can find his latest standup  comedy special on Amazon Prime, his feature films in various languages and motivational talks on Youtube, live theatre productions nowhere but live, and his first book, in your hands right now.

In *Don't Startup,* he recounts the journey of going into an unknown area as an entrepreneur and the challenges posed in this voyage of business and self-discovery.

Evam was founded in 2003 by two amateur theatre enthusiasts and marketing postgraduates, to be India's first full-fledged theatre-based self-funded organization.

The founders had no pedigree in the arts and entrepreneurship didn't run in their blood. They heard several well-meaning people telling them, 'Don't Startup!' They did nonetheless.

Fifteen years hence, Evam is now a rare white elephant, in the Indian entrepreneurship space, with businesses in theatre performance, Standup Comedy, Behavioural Corporate Training, Children's Education, Brand Activation Using Theatre, Digital Storytelling and Performing Arts and Artist Management. The headquarters is based out of Chennai with operations in most major cities in India, and also touring properties across USA, UK, Australia, Singapore, to name a few. Evam is proof of what can be done with the arts within a solid entrepreneurial Management eco system, and more so of what can get achieved when you set off on what appears like an impossible journey.

Log on to **www.evam.in** to know more about Evam's journey and services.

Made in the USA
Middletown, DE
04 March 2019